Perennials
Short *and* Tall

Perennials
Short *and* Tall

A Seasonal Progression of

Flowers for Your

Garden

Bleeding Heart
Dicentra spectabilis

Moya L. Andrews

Illustrated by Gillian Harris

AN IMPRINT OF
Indiana University Press
BLOOMINGTON AND INDIANAPOLIS

This book is a publication of

Indiana University Press
601 North Morton Street
Bloomington, IN
47404-3797 USA

http://iupress.indiana.edu

Telephone orders   800-842-6796
Fax orders   812-855-7931
Orders by e-mail   iuporder@indiana.edu

Manufactured in China

See page 146 for Library of Congress
Cataloging-in-Publication data.

1 2 3 4 5 13 12 11 10 09 08

A NOTE ABOUT ZONES . . .

Although this book often refers to "the Midwest
garden," the perennials profiled thrive in many
of North America's hardiness zones.
Please see the USDA Plant Hardiness Zone Map
on page 140 to determine which zone is yours.
The headnote for each plant specifies the
zones in which it can be cultivated.

THE FRAGRANCE

OF FLOWERS

STAYS IN THE HANDS

OF THOSE

WHO GIVE THEM.

Chinese proverb

Contents

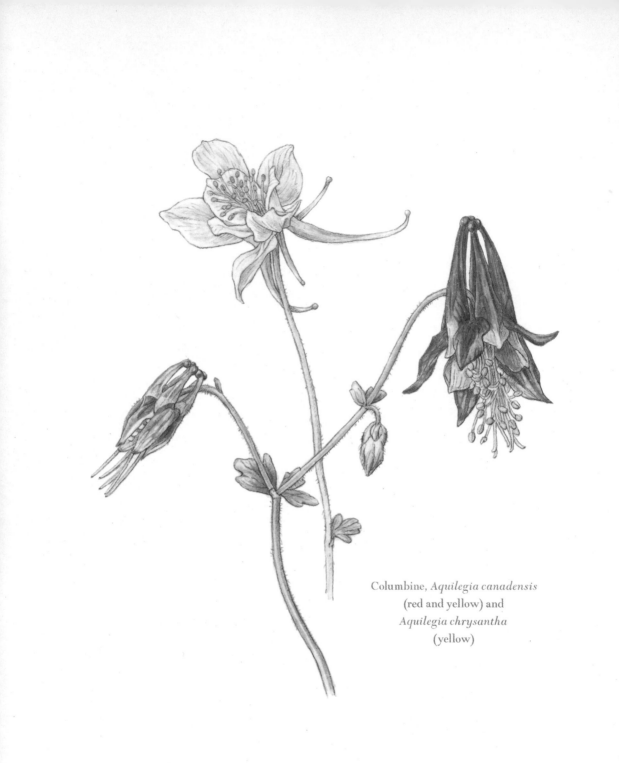

Columbine, *Aquilegia canadensis*
(red and yellow) and
Aquilegia chrysantha
(yellow)

Illustrations

Lavender

Lavandula angustifolia

Preface

What a desolate place would be
a world without flowers!
It would be a face without a smile,
a feast without a welcome.

——Clara Balfour

These words resonate with all who love flowers. Flowers are not a luxury for us, they are a necessity, and they provide a kind of anticipatory structure in our lives. We look forward to the appearance of the varied types of flowers in our gardens, and treasure their arrival in the same way we treasure the reappearance of dear friends. Each winter we await the early spring flowers with excitement that is palpable. Knowing the impermanence of each individual flower does not daunt us. It just makes us savor their special time with us, as we gaze at them hoping to imprint them in our memory.

We know that perennial flowers recur in the predictable cycle of the seasons. And so it is that across the entire growing season we enjoy the succession of bloom, secure in the knowledge of the unfolding sequence. Our dream is that at all times during the growing season, we will be able to step out into our gardens and find flowers to pick. We collect containers to suit the demands of all sizes and types of flowers and we imagine just how they will look, and where we will place our bouquets in our homes. When winter weather robs us of the instant gratification of flowers from our own gardens, we look forward to having outdoor flowers again, and prepare houseplants that bloom indoors. We purchase flowers for Thanksgiving, for the holidays, and for Valentine's Day. Every seasonal event is an opportunity for the flower lover. Seasons and events have heightened meaning for us because of the flowers associated with them.

This book is about the integral part flowers play in our lives and their meaning, not only in our age, but in ages past. Each family of flowers has its own history and peculiarities, just as human families do. Flowering plants' pedigrees and stories are fascinating, and knowing about them increases the depth of the relationship each of us has with our own plants. Time is inextricably woven into the fabric of gardening as the destiny of all flowers is anchored in the seasons. And since the seasons occur at different times dependent on hemispheres, there are always flowers blooming somewhere in the world.

As already noted, flowers are the focus of this book and we will discuss perennial plants that flourish in areas with cold winters, where their roots must withstand sub-freezing temperatures. We will describe perennial flower gardening with special attention to zones 4 through 7 on the USDA Hardiness Zone Map. Of course, since a perennial is by definition a plant that survives for at least three years, the term has different connotations in different areas of the United States. Plants that live for only one growing season in areas with cold winters, for example, may be perennial in regions with winter temperatures that stay above freezing.

Perennial plants form an eclectic group. Some are tall and others are short, and their heights, in addition to their other distinctive features, add variety to gardens. We will take their habits as well as their requirements into account and provide advice on how and where to plant them so they settle in, thrive, and provide a progression of bloom.

We have also profiled twenty-five of the best perennials that grow in the Midwest and perform reliably for both experienced and novice gardeners. These are described and illustrated in chapters 5 through 7. You will learn about where these stalwart plants come from and how to make them feel at home in your own garden. The book closes with twenty-two appendices. Here you will find lists of drought-tolerant plants, plants with grey foliage, flowers to plant in the fall, tall and short plants, flowers that bloom in the shade, blue and pink and orange flowers, tips on choosing the best site, and more.

Facing page: Forget-me-not, *Brunnera macrophylla*

Perennials
Short *and* Tall

Peony

Paeonia lactiflora

ONE

An Inviting Garden

Won't you come into my garden?
I want my roses to see you.
—*Richard Sheridan*

Those of us who love flowers, to an extent that other people might find hard to understand, have an intimate relationship with them. This relationship deepens as we ourselves mature and learn more about their distinctive features and how they impact us. We may start out responding to their colors, shapes, and forms, sensing that we feel something quite special in their presence. Perhaps we then begin to recognize the other attributes that particularly delight us, and yearn for flowers that have special perfumes, or ones that evoke memories of people or of places that were meaningful to us in our childhood or times past. At some point in our evolving understanding of the significant part that flowers play in our existence, we realize that flowers really are an essential aspect of our identity, and they can affect how we actually feel day by day.

We realize that they serve as our symbols of the seasons. We wait to see the first spring flowers each year and we feel a deep need to mark each event by savoring the flowers that are associated with special times. We look for the daffodils in the spring, Easter lilies at Easter, poinsettias at Christmas, and so on. Also, instead of just waiting hopefully for someone to give us flowers, we come to the understanding that they are essential to our well-being. So we become more proactive in seeking out opportunities to have flowers. At this point we usually give ourselves permission to buy flowers for ourselves. Fortunately, nowadays flowers are available year-round, and it is a happy thing for us since we can so easily pick up our favorites and pop them into our grocery carts as we shop for food. Flowers, we have come to understand, are indeed food for our souls.

Flower growing has become a huge forty-billion-dollar industry worldwide. Greenhouse growers have perfected techniques that precisely adjust the timing of when plants bloom to meet market demands. Air transport of flowers grown outdoors in the Southern Hemisphere ensures their availability for Northern Hemisphere consumers all through our winters. Scientific advances and both horticultural and aeronautical practices allow us to indulge ourselves year-round. There is no time of the year nowadays when we don't have access to cut flowers.

However, no flowers we purchase seem to evoke exactly the same feelings as those we grow in our own gardens. The process of gardening, and the contexts we create, make our home-grown flowers more personal. So, inevitably for many of us, as we deepen our connection with flowers, we become more interested in gardening. It is a logical next step in the development of self-reliance in understanding and meeting our own needs. Sometimes this is deferred because of circumstances. We may have to wait until we have a house with a yard or until the children are older and we have more discretionary time and money. However, as time and opportunity allow, we eventually begin to grow more of our own flowers.

Those of us who have a passion for flowers always want to grow as many as possible. However, in the beginning of our evolution as gardeners, we may plant only annuals. These plants, which flower continuously across one growing season and then die when the first killing frost occurs, provide a wealth of exuberant color and can be tucked into beds or pots and nooks and crannies near our homes. However, in time, most flower lovers realize the benefits of expanding their plant repertoire to include perennials. These plants do not bloom continuously all season as annuals do, it is true; however, by planting a number of different perennials we can always have some flowers in bloom throughout the entire growing season.

MORE THAN ONE NAME

Perennials Are Herbaceous

Herbaceous perennials have soft top growth that dies to the ground each winter. In this way they are different from shrubs, which have woody stems that stay bare of leaves but erect above ground. When herbaceous perennials, shrubs, and perennial bulbs are planted together in a garden it is possible to orchestrate an uninterrupted display of flowers. It starts with the first spring bulbs, progresses through the abundance of summer, and ends the growing season with a glorious fall finale. The attainment of perfect continuity is similar to the experience of finding the Holy Grail for perennial gardeners. Each plant blooms briefly at its appointed time, and many overlap, but all are an integral part of the serendipity of well-executed perennial gardens.

Pass-Along Plants

One of the traditions of perennial gardening is the ancient practice of passing plants along from one garden to another. Although plants have roots, they are also nomads. When we start our perennial gardens, most of us, if we are fortunate, inherit some of these pass-along plants. As all gardeners learn, you first have no perennials, and then suddenly, because some are so prolific, you have lots. Gardeners cannot bear to waste treasured plants, and so as they divide those that grow vigorously, they pass them along to others. It is an endearing habit, and a habit that is an inextricable part of a committed gardener's identity. Gardeners are among the world's most generous and sharing people. They believe deeply in recycling and sustainability. They share a reverence for, and a profound bond with, their environment.

After a while, however, new gardeners start to look beyond plants they have inherited from others. It is then that they become serious customers of local garden centers and mail order catalogs. More unusual plants beckon as the quest to have something always in bloom intensifies. In order to be selective shoppers, however, we need to understand more about the names of plants.

Plant Nomenclature

Plants often have many common names, and it is not unusual for the same plant to have different names in different regions. So, informal common names, while frequently picturesque and fun, are not necessarily reliable when a gardener is searching for a specific plant. We need to know the formal names. This is analogous to knowing people's given names in addition to their nicknames. When we delve into the formal botanical system of naming plants, we find that, like people, plants have more than one name. People have given names as well as surnames, and surnames denote their lineage—that is, who their parents were. It is somewhat similar with plants. Each plant has a pedigree name (a genus) and each has a specific name that distinguishes it from other family members (a species name). Plants' names differ from many people's names, though, in that their genus name comes first and the individual name comes second. A Swedish naturalist, Carl Linnaeus (1707–1778), designed the classification system that is still used today.

Prior to Linnaeus, plants had been organized in large groups according to their structural characteristics. Then they were each assigned to a smaller group called a *genus* (plural *genera*). Linnaeus broke each of the genera into smaller entities called *species,* and he used Latin but also some Greek and other names to describe each plant's characteristics. Botanical Latin is somewhat different from classical Latin, though of course knowledge of classical Latin is extremely helpful in understanding the names of plants we encounter today. However, it is not essential and most of us can manage fairly well if we understand just a few basic guidelines to help us decipher what plant names really mean. Basically Linnaeus designed botanical shorthand, and in giving each plant both a genus name and a species name, Linnaeus developed a binomial (two-word) system. The genus name is capitalized and is a singular noun, and the lowercase species name is a descriptive adjective which agrees with the noun in terms of case and number. Thus *Iris siberica* is an iris from Siberia, and when it is written the genus will be denoted by the capital letter and the species will be written out in lowercase in full (e.g., *I. siberica*). Sometimes there is a third Latin name if there is a subspecies or naturally occurring variety. But usually we are more likely to see a cultivar name following the species name. Cultivars and hybrids are the result of human intervention in the reproductive activity of plants.

Hybridizers have developed many new cultivars which they usually name in English, and these names are written capitalized in single quotation marks. For example, *I. siberica* 'Caesar's Brother' is an old award-winning variety of Siberian iris which many of us have in our gardens and cherish for its rich purple coloring and exceptional vigor in zones 3–8. White Flower Farm Catalog (www.whiteflowerfarm.com) also advertises what is referred to as "an important color breakthrough in Siberian Iris breeding, due to a Currier McEwan cross." It is an iris with bright yellow falls (petals that droop) and white standards (upright petals). This hybrid has been aptly named *I. siberica* 'Butter and Sugar', and so we know the genus and species (with origin) and that human intervention was involved, as well as the fact that it is a bi-color since the flower colors are yellow and white. This example illustrates how well the system Linnaeus devised so brilliantly actually works. It is brief, concise, and descriptive. In this particular example, the cultivar name told us a great deal, but that is not always the case. More frequently it is the species name that provides the most information. The species can tell us such things as whether the plant is very tall (*giganteus*), tall (*altus*), large (*macro*), small (*micro*), or dwarf (*nanus; humilis*). It tells us if it creeps (*repens* or *reptans*), and if it has recurved petals (*recurvus*) or if the leaves are like the palm of a hand (*palmatum*). The species name presents descriptive information based on the plant's essential and distinctive features, and that information is useful in providing identification of the plant because those characteristics will continue to persist across successive generations. There are very exact rules provided by the International Code of Nomenclature concerning the way species are named.

When I have a question about plant names, I refer to *Hortus Third* (1976) to help me understand the meaning and classification. For example, in that volume I find that *cultivar* is a word that evolved from "cultivated variety." When cultivars seed, their offspring will not be true to their parents. You may have noticed this in your garden. For example, *Brunnera macrophylla* (perennial forget-me-not or Siberian bugloss) has a cultivar, 'Jack Frost', which has silver leaves, but its self-seeded offspring will all revert to the species' green leaves. Cultivar names are chosen names, and so are obviously different from the Latin botanical names. The cultivar's name, while always capitalized, may also be preceded by the abbreviation *cv*. The names of hybrid plants, which are crosses, are preceded by the multiplication sign (×). When this sign is read aloud, however, it is not pronounced as the symbol would be in other contexts. Rather the phrase "the hybrid species" is substituted. Thus, to describe a hypothetical cross of New York and New England asters the following could be written: "*A. novi-belgii* × *novae-angliae* 'Evening'"; this could be spoken aloud as: "'Evening' is a late-blooming hybrid aster resulting from a cross between the New York and New England asters species."

Endings of Botanical Names

Within genera there are distinct plant families and these can often be recognized by the ending *-aceae* attached to the stem of the name of the genus. Consider *Violaceae*, which is the family name for violets. *Viol* is the genus name and the suffix *-aceae* is added to it. In the profiles of individual perennials that appear later in this book, beginning on page 61, you will see the family name of each of the perennials pictured. Genus names are primarily Latin or Greek words but may be words borrowed from other languages. However, generic names are always treated as if they are Latin, regardless of their linguistic origin. So the ending of the word for the genus dictates the ending of the word for the species. For example, the endings for both genus and species are masculine in *Lupinus albus*, and because the noun indicating the *Lupin* genus ends in *-us*, the adjective indicating it is white must end in a similar way. If the noun signifying the genus was feminine it would, as would the species name, end in *-a*. In the case of a neuter genus name, such as *Sedum album*, the species name acquires a neuter (*-um*) ending. When a species is named after a person, however, and the name ends in a vowel, an *-i* is added at the end of that word. If the name ends in a consonant, two (*-ii*) are added. So the purple clematis developed by the Jackman family is *C. Jackmanii* (pronounced JACK-man-eye). If a name ends in an *a*, however, an *-e* is added; thus, the name Balansa becomes *Balansae*.

Common names are an important part of our horticultural heritage and some are whimsical, as in the case of *Lycoris squamigera*, which is a summer-blooming bulb with pink flowers borne aloft on leafless stems. It is commonly referred to as a "naked lady." However, there are also some common names that have merely been adopted from the name of the genus, most notably iris and narcissus.

Many of the plants and herbs used in ancient times for medicinal purposes ended in the suffix *-wort*. This comes from the old English word for *root*, which was *wyrt*. Herbalists in medieval times developed a theory known as the doctrine of signatures. This theory described how the external forms of herbs and plants provided clues concerning which part of a diseased human body could be cured using medicines made from the plants' roots, flowers, or leaves. *Hepatica* (liverwort) has leaves that look like human livers, and so was used for liver conditions. *Pulmonaria* (lungwort) has spotted leaves thought to resemble diseased lungs. Some plants were thought to belong to the sun and some to the moon, and others belonged to planets. Flowers of the sun were used for headaches. Culinary herbs have always been used to flavor food, and sage (*Salvia officinalis*) was also used as a drink, a gargle, and a hair wash, and the Romans were especially devoted to its use and carried it with them to distant lands. Many plants were named because of their resemblance to birds and animals (lamb's ears, for instance). *Columba* means dove and *Aquilegia* means eagle in Latin, and the columbine (*Aquilegia vulgaris*) has petals with spurred tips like an eagle while the flower petals themselves look like five doves sitting in a circle. "Granny's bonnet" is a very descriptive common name also given to columbine.

Plants that turn to follow the movement of the sun are described as *helio-tropic*, from the Greek word *helios*, meaning the sun. Thus one finds the word *helianthus* in the names of many of these types of plants. The loveliest common names are the evocative ones such as "love-in-a-mist," which was one of Gertrude Jekyll's favorite flowers. While it is an annual for us, it self-seeds and thus often persists well in our gardens.

While Shakespeare wrote, "that which we call a rose / By any other name would smell as sweet," names are important for correct identification of plants. Not only do we want to find exactly what we want to buy, but we want to ensure that the plant's pedigree and habits will match our own garden's needs. Thus, some knowledge of plant classifications, and the meanings embodied in their names, helps us read plant catalogs and labels more effectively so that we can make informed selections. Fortunately, when we shop at nurseries in our own region, we can often obtain help from trained personnel who can provide additional information.

LIGHT AND TEMPERATURE

Plants need light, and different species of plants have differing requirements about the type of light they need. The length of each day and how this changes during the year also dramatically impacts plants. The amount of daylight a region experiences determines the pattern of vegetative growth, initiation and development of flowering, and enticement to dormancy. Plants survive in a region of the country, or specifically in a certain zone, only if the day-length promotes their growth to maturity and also prepares them for the approaching seasonal changes. Plants also grow best within the range of temperatures that is optimal for their species. While some species can adapt and thrive within a wide range of temperatures, other species require a temperature range that is quite narrow. Plants must be able to metabolize, and their species determines the range of temperatures necessary for them to accomplish this important task.

Related to day-length and temperature range is tolerance to frost and to freezing. Plants differ in their ability to survive frost and while some may react with immediate death, some can sustain life because their species can tolerate freezing or sub-freezing temperatures. Hardy perennials that tolerate sub-freezing temperatures have root systems that remain viable even after the above-ground vegetative part of the plant dies down.

Temperature Cut-Offs

The cut-off temperatures for both cold and hot extremes vary widely from species to species. The length of time that plants are exposed to temperatures near to or beyond their cut-offs also plays a part. Long periods of extremes of either cold or heat near or beyond a species' cut-off obviously affect the plants' chances of survival. Additionally, the site a plant occupies can sometimes mitigate its response to temperature extremes. We traditionally categorize plants as sun, partial sun, partial shade, or shade types according to their tolerance for light and heat.

Perennials planted in a zone that experiences temperatures right at the limit of their range may sometimes survive if they are in a protected spot. That may be, for example, a location that provides shade from afternoon sun, for a sun-loving plant in a zone where temperatures may intermittently exceed its thermal cut-off. Or, conversely, a site near the foundation of a house, that provides warmth and protection from wind, for a plant in a zone where temperatures may on occasion dip below its cold tolerance.

In areas with see-sawing temperatures, above and below freezing in the spring, some plants will be affected by the temperature fluctuation more than others. Those that cannot tolerate it may survive, however, if planted on the north side of a structure where the sun does not entice them to break dormancy too soon. The shade from the structure may keep their soil cold enough that they may hibernate longer.

Interacting Variables

Many environmental factors interact and contribute to the survival as well as the level of performance of our perennials. Soil type influences the ability of plants to take up water and nutrients, and this depends on the soil's pH, which is a measure of relative acidity or alkalinity. Plants are also affected by the presence of soluble salts and the looseness or aeration of the soil. Wind, moisture, and winter sunshine and amount of snow, as well as summer humidity, can greatly influence how perennials adapt in our gardens. For example, winter snow cover provides an insulating blanket for the roots of plants, so that in areas where there is continuous snow cover during winter, roots actually are sometimes better protected than they are in regions where snow cover is intermittent.

Plant Hardiness

Plants can adapt to a range of conditions and environments, but it is desirable for gardeners to have accurate information to help them select the plants that will not only survive but flourish in their own regions. Consequently, the USDA Hardiness Zone Map was developed under the supervision of Henry T.

Skinner, the second director of the U.S. National Arboretum. He cooperated with the American Horticulturalist Society and with horticultural scientists to ensure that accurate and meaningful meteorological and horticultural information was condensed into an accessible system. A map of the contiguous United States and Canada was developed and color coded into ten zones, each separated by a difference of 10°F in average annual minimum temperatures. The zone ratings for plants were based primarily on winter survival. This was judged to be the most important criterion of their adaptability to an environment. Zone ratings were also based on plants' adaptability and ability to flourish, not merely to survive.

Perennial plants and seeds are classified, however, to indicate the areas where the plants will survive *both* winter and summer temperatures. Plant tags at nurseries provide this information for each perennial plant. To match the plants' requirements with the area in which we garden, we can go to www .usna.usda.gov and click on the USDA Plant Hardiness Zone Map link, which is found near the bottom of the homepage. This interactive map helps gardeners determine their gardens' zones. The zone map also appears on page 140 of this book. It is interesting for us, when on a car trip driving north or south in the spring, to see the way the flowers that are in bloom change as we drive through different zones. Generally speaking, each one hundred miles causes a change in bloom time by about one week.

Microclimates

In addition to understanding how to match plants to the zone temperatures in which we garden, we also need to understand the microclimates that occur on our own property. As we have already seen, plants have different requirements for light and shade as well as moisture, and since perennials will hopefully be permanent residents in our gardens, it is worth remembering that we will have more numerous flowers if we site them appropriately after we first obtain them either from nurseries or as divisions from plants in friends' gardens. In addition to the general climate in which we live, there are variations in the climate within our own property. These variations are small yet often significant in terms of the best site for particular plants. For instance, if we live in a region which experiences extremes in terms of both cold and hot temperatures we will need to take this into consideration with respect to exposure to sun, protection from wind, and freezing and thawing in late winter and spring and so on. This may be especially important in making our selections, too. If we garden in regions of the Midwest with extremely cold winters, we may be tempted to specialize in Canadian-bred roses that are especially cold-tolerant. However, Canadian roses may not prosper if we have humid, hot summers. In such cases we may want to consider those bred by Professor Griffith Buck, who developed cultivars such as the pink 'Carefree Beauty', 'Carefree Wonder', and 'Barn Dance' and the apricot 'Maytime' to withstand the climate in his state of Iowa. Dr. Buck, who worked at Iowa State University, bred roses that may be seen in Reiman Gardens, a public garden in Ames, Iowa. He bred seventy-five varieties that grow well in the Midwest. They tolerate cold in zones 4 and 5 without protection, as well as shrugging off hot, humid summers. All roses need at least six hours of sun a day, however, regardless of the temperatures in a specific region. Even the more recently developed disease-resistant cultivars such as the Knock Out landscape roses, which require less care, still need appropriate sunshine.

Generally speaking, perennials that need full sun should be planted where they get eight hours of direct sun. Some native perennials, such as yellow sunflower varieties and purple coneflowers, withstand and even seem to enjoy unrelenting hot sun in summer and tolerate dry soil. However, some other sun-loving perennials like some shade in summer afternoons and must have thick mulch to help retain moisture in the soil. Perennials that are described as needing partial shade still need strong filtered light. Deciduous trees can provide this type of light if their lower branches are removed so that only the higher branches provide their leaf canopy. This process of "limbing up" a tree also frequently makes the tree trunk look more graceful and has the added benefit of making it easier for the gardener to move around when gardening in a bed surrounding the trunk. Morning sun is preferable to sun in the afternoon, which is usually hotter.

Dappled shade is ideal for many plants where summers are extremely hot. Maples have matted shallow roots that make it difficult to dig in the soil nearby, but other deciduous trees with deep roots provide enough surface soil and excellent dappled shade if they have been limbed up. A garden under trees of this kind can be a good location for spring bulbs, since bulbs bloom and die down before the trees completely leaf out. The spring display of bulbs can be followed by low-growing perennials such as celandine poppy, *Brunnera*, *Epimedium*, *Heuchera*, *Dicentra*, *Pulmonaria*, and *Astilbe*. Deep shade, such as that cast by evergreens, is more challenging, since it is dense and even shade lovers do not enjoy restricted light. Such a site may work, however, as a location for those cheerful early-blooming little bulbs that need to be placed somewhere where they won't inadvertently be disturbed once their foliage has died down. An out-of-the-way spot under an evergreen is not a place we are likely to choose for something else, so they are less likely to be disturbed by our digging around. Dry shade is always problematic, but low-growing epimedium and lamium, once established, will tolerate such conditions, as will the more aggressive ferns and hostas as long as the gardener can tolerate the crispy dry leaves they will develop if they do not get much moisture in high summer.

The longer one gardens the more one understands the subtle variations in conditions in one's own garden. For example, the south side of a property warms up in the spring earlier than the north side, and slopes and raised beds provide better drainage for plants than do low-lying areas. Close observation over time teaches us a lot as we garden. Also the more we read about gardening and about the origins of the plants we grow, the more adept we become at choosing appropriate sites to match each plant's needs. For example, once we learn that many lavenders originated in a Mediterranean climate, we better understand why they dislike wet feet and thrive on slopes and in raised beds. It takes some trial and error before we master concepts such as the interaction between the way soil drains and/or the way the moisture soaks into the soil, and the provision of sufficient moisture relative to rainfall and to changes in the temperature, and respond appropriately by siting plants in the best spot for them.

PREPARATION AND PLANTING

While we often read about the importance of amending the soil in our gardens, at first we sometimes just put plants into whatever soil we have and hope for the best. Many perennials, especially natives to our region, may cope quite well with this approach. However, as we garden over the years, we will observe that to get the best results we need to amend the soil. Thus we develop tricks such as adding organic matter each time we dig a hole and using some of the following time-honored techniques:

• Examine a plug of soil, and have a soil test done to determine the pH and other characteristics of your soil. Clay soil is heavy and is more difficult for small roots to penetrate, but it does have the advantage of retaining moisture. Sandy soil offers better root penetration (and is easier to dig), but water drains through it so rapidly that roots dry out very quickly.

• Work organic matter such as peat moss and compost into the soil regularly, beginning ideally when you first dig a new bed or border. Soil that is high in organic matter is loose and drains well, yet retains a certain amount of moisture also. Most perennials prefer a neutral pH or one that is slightly on the acid side, though many will adapt to more alkaline conditions.

• Mulch your garden with compost or organic materials such as chopped leaves, shredded bark, or cocoa shells. Organic mulches break down over time and are worked into the soil as we dig holes for new plants. Be careful about walking on your beds, as this compacts the soil, reducing the air spaces that the roots need and thus canceling out the beneficial effects of the organic material.

• Outline the shape and size and proportions of a new bed by using a garden hose to define and adjust perimeters before preparing the area.

• Start preparing a new bed in the fall using a method such as spreading a thick layer of soaking wet newspapers over the area, then covering them with piles of leaves or other organic mulch. Then water well and allow the area to rest over the winter months. When spring comes and you begin to plant, the newspapers will have broken down and the bed will have settled.

• Use a technique such as single digging, which involves spreading compost over a bed and turning shovelfuls of soil over, or double digging, which involves trenching to incorporate the compost into a new area. Double digging is advocated in many books on gardening and is the best option if your back will withstand the strain or if you have access to a helper with a strong back and generous disposition.

• Do not work the soil when the area is either too dry or too wet. Overly wet soil, when dug, makes huge clumps, and overly dry soil will leave you covered in dust. Dry soil can always be watered a day or so before you plan to work it, but with overly wet soil, no matter how eager you are to get started, you will just have to exercise patience until the soil dries out and crumbles when you take a handful instead of forming a muddy clump in your palm.

• Monitor the progress of your soil improvement program by noting whether there is an increase in the number of earthworms. The best loam is alive with billions of microorganisms and other small creatures. When organic matter such as peat, grass clippings, leaves, straw, and compost is added to sand, silt, or clay, the fertility as well as the texture of the soil improves along with the activity of earthworms, making the soil look and feel more like loam. In gardening terms we describe this kind of soil as "friable."

Beds and Borders

When we are planning a perennial garden, it is instructive to read about the work of the famous English designer Gertrude Jekyll (1843–1932). She designed and popularized herbaceous borders full of English cottage garden perennials. She believed that flowers that bloom at the same time should be planted close to each other, so that there is a mass of color rather than bits of color scattered around a garden. She was a painter by training and said that no color stands alone and that a color has value only if it is seen and thought of in relation to the colors close beside it. She wrote about the impossibility of having continuous color across an entire garden at one time and believed that groups of colorfully blooming plants are enhanced by the foliage of the plants that are not currently in bloom. She also advocated the use of monochromatic gardens that combined many variations of only one color: blues, golds, or reds, for example. She emphasized the importance of using grey foliage to soften the patterns of colors in borders and she cherished fragrance in the garden. Her work as a garden designer and writer has profoundly influenced the way perennial gardens have evolved on both sides of the Atlantic. She advocated planting three rather than one of each type of herbaceous perennial (plants with roots that winter over so that soft herbaceous top growth recurs each spring). She liked beds with plants that seem woven together so that there appear to be drifts of color.

Generally speaking, the word "border" is applied to beds that have a backdrop such as a wall or fence. Tall plants are placed at the back, with medium-height plants in the middle and low-growing plants in the front. "Bed" is used when a garden is created without a structural backdrop. A bed might be edged on opposite sides by paths, for example, and short plants will be grown on both sides, with taller plants along the center of plantings.

The concept of island beds, surrounded on all sides by a grass lawn, was developed and popularized by Alan Bloom at Bressingham Nursery, near the city of Norwich in England, in the early 1950s. It occurred to him that perennials would do better in freestanding beds so light and air as well as access would be maximized. Bloom's island beds proved easy to make because he used the then–newly available mechanical dozers and bucket excavators to mechanize the process. Bloom's garden, now operated by his son, Adrian, is still open to the public and is well worth a visit. Island beds are usually round or kidney-shaped and edged by short plants around their perimeter. Taller perennials and grasses form a spine in the center, much like a mountain range in the middle of an actual island in the sea. Medium-sized plants are placed between the tall and low-growing plantings. Large island beds in big expanses of lawn may also have small trees or tall shrubs as focal points in their centers. A bed where the soil is piled high is called a berm.

Multi-Seasonal Plantings

In small gardens with only one large bed or several small beds, many gardeners design plantings so that some perennials are always in bloom in each site. English gardeners excel in creating these multi-seasonal plantings that provide a cottage garden effect. The perennials are often augmented with flowering shrubs and short annuals that weave around the base of taller perennials and also edge the beds. However, the short hardy cranesbill geraniums, lady's mantle, dianthus, non-flowering lamb's ears, saponaria, and catmint can be used to fill this role, if a garden is dedicated entirely to perennial plantings.

Single-Season Plantings

Gardeners with large spaces may decide to dedicate individual beds or borders to seasonally specific gardens often referred to as single-season gardens. Instead of aiming to have something always in bloom in each bed, they decide to let the focus of attention move from bed to bed as the growing season progresses. One bed may be dedicated to a succession of spring bulbs and early-flowering low-growing perennials, such as creeping phlox, saponaria, and candytuft, that combine well with bulbs. Or the spring bulbs can be interplanted with daylilies. This is a popular combination, as the daylilies grow up just at the time their foliage is needed to provide camouflage for the bulb foliage as it dies down. Another popular combination is German irises and peonies that bloom at the same time. A flower bed that peaks in high summer might include such plants as monarda, coneflower, Shasta daisies, globe thistle, Russian sage, and malva as the tall specimens, edged with grey lamb's ears and catmint or low sedums.

Mail order plant catalogs and garden magazines are good sources of inspiration with regard to plant selections that ensure continuity of bloom. Another source of inspiration for gardeners who wish to find plants that suit their own geographic area and provide staggered periods of bloom is to borrow ideas from other gardeners in their own neighborhoods. Find a garden that you especially admire and drive by or, better still, walk by regularly, all through the growing season. Each time a plant that you admire blooms, check your catalog to identify it from the pictures and add its name to your own wish list. Many perennials are easy to acquire from other gardeners, but others are only available to purchase, either locally or through the mail. One way to meet other flower gardeners, who may have perennials they are dividing, is to join a local gardening club or enroll in a Master Gardeners program. As well as learning more about gardening you will be able to network with other gardeners who have information to share about perennials that grow well in your zone.

Aspects of Harmonious Design

Gardens are more than just collections of plants, however. The overall effect of the design of a garden must be harmonious. Since each plant spends more time out of bloom than it does in bloom, it must also provide additional pleasing elements: leaf size and characteristics, the shape and form of the entire plant, and a plant's usefulness in terms of accent and contrast all contribute to the overall effect.

Plants such as *Ligularia* that have big glossy leaves contrast with plants with small leaves. Succulents such as tall sedums, with fleshy heavy leaves and large flower heads, provide texture that contrasts with airy, ferny-leaved plants such as Russian sage. When we can't find enough color or texture in perennial plantings, we can also add a few annuals. For example, annual salvia provides deep blues that supplement the orangey and red colors that often dominate the fall landscape. We must always be thinking of the overall design of our garden and be alert to individual plants that can provide additional interest by either echoing or contrasting with existing shapes, colors, forms, and textures in different areas of our gardens. However, we should try to ensure that all of the elements are threaded together so that there are enough connections to provide a harmonious overall design. Also, the garden must be appropriate to the style, color, and architectural motifs of the home. For example, palladium windows may be echoed in rounded arches placed in the garden.

One of the more recent trends in garden design is the use of naturalistic drifts of grasses, native perennials, and foliage plants demonstrated by designers such as Piet Oudolf of the Netherlands and referred to as the New Wave approach. These types of plantings create a tapestry of textures. Texture and pattern that can be savored at all seasons of the year are important aspects of design. The texture of the bark of trees, too, is a significant element. Garden hardscape (structural items such as paths, walls, and pergolas), furniture, accessories, and ornaments, made of materials such as wood and stone, add a feeling of permanence to a landscape by anchoring the more transitory natural elements, and also provide winter interest. The emotional impact of a garden, whether it is restful or stimulating, restrained or expansive, contemplative or energizing, is determined by the relationships of line, plane, pattern, and type and number of decorative objects. The intertwining of the form and functions inherent in the garden, the transition between the house and garden, and the way the hard elements and the softer plantings are melded together contribute to the overall response we have to a garden.

The choice between tall or short plants and where they are placed is a crucial aspect of design. The vertical versus the horizontal is a design imperative which contributes to the overarching need for balance. Height, width, and depth are components of balance, as are symmetry and asymmetry. Balance must be achieved in relation to structures as well as to plantings, of course. Consider some of the following aspects which are pertinent to residential garden design.

CURVES VERSUS STRAIGHT LINES

The architecture of the home, as well as the level of informality or formality, influences the lines in the garden. The geometry of horizontal planes, such as rectilinear areas of lawn or plantings versus curved ones, should echo the lines or motifs of the home. The way edges of beds and thresholds between areas are handled will also contribute to the coherence and flow of the garden.

MINIMALISM VERSUS ABUNDANCE

Whether a garden overflows with plants, or plants are selected and placed for individual effect, depends on the taste of the gardener. A few items strategically placed, a narrow versus a wide palette of plants, and the rhythm and repetition of the grouping will contribute to the formality and/or minimalism of the design. Plants that are used for their vertical sculptural impact (such as *Kniphofia*, large hostas, tall sedums, and yucca) may be used as accents or massed depending on the desired effect. Or they may be repeated symmetrically or asymmetrically.

ACTIVITY VERSUS SERENITY

Sights, sounds, and the motion of birds, hummingbirds, and insects may be empha-sized in a garden. Water may be used to create energy or restfulness. For example, a reflecting pool creates a completely different effect from that produced by a fountain or a waterfall. Shrubs and trees may provide nesting places for birds, and plantings can be selected to provide nectar for hummingbirds, butterflies, and beneficial insects. Birdbaths and bird feeders can be strategically placed and used as the theme for garden ornaments. Plant colors may be bold to be inviting for hummingbirds, and a wide variety of different plants can be used. Conversely, if the aim is to have a serene design, a narrow range of plants and colors may be selected, or the plant colors may be restricted only to shades of green or grey with soothing colors as accents. Or the color palette of the garden could be restricted to those colors that harmonize with those of the house. The relative proportion of plantings to hardscape can also be ad-justed to create specific effects. The solidity of various types of stone, the contrasting colors of pebbles and stones, and the scale of individual items can also contribute to the level of serenity evoked. Plant colors, textures, and shapes that echo or contrast with the colors, shapes, and textures of the accessories will also contribute to the feel-ing of restfulness or vibrancy. Formal garden rooms, clipped hedges, and columnar trees will be more restful than a meadow of wildflowers and grasses that rustle in the breeze and provide a magnet for winged creatures. The spiky leaves of plants such as iris and the chartreuse foliage of *Liriope muscari* 'Pee Dee Ingot' might be used intermittently in a garden full of activity or in swathes or as accents in a formal or serene setting. So the same plants, used in different ways, will be equally at home in all types of gardens. It is the way they contribute to the overall organization of the garden that will be significant in terms of design.

In the appendices there are plant lists that identify short and tall perennials that bloom well at specific seasons and can be incorporated into both single-season and multi-seasonal beds, and into formal or naturalistic plantings. In subsequent chapters and in the plant profiles you will also find descriptions of reliable plants that may meet your garden's requirements, and also appeal to you.

TWO

Work in Progress

Flower gardens are reflections
of their creators.
A garden, as well as the gardener,
is always a work in progress.

ach garden is unique, and it is never the same—day by day, season by season, year by year. Part of the joy of creating a garden is the continual sense of anticipation that comes as a result of partnering with Mother Nature, who is full of surprises. The process of raising flowers is itself instructive. Claude Monet said that perhaps he owed his becoming a painter to flowers. We expand our perceptions of colors, forms, shapes, perfumes, and permutations and combinations. We keep learning about design and elements of style through the medium of gardening. Change is inevitable. Established trees are uprooted by storms and shade gardens are transformed into sun gardens. Small trees mature and sun gardens are engulfed in shade. Water restrictions force us to investigate drought-tolerant plants. A visit to Vita Sackville-West's garden at Sissinghurst, in England, moves us to create our own white garden. Whatever shifts in motivation and circumstances occur, there are perennials we can find to create the effects we need. We continually augment our collection, redesign beds to combine plants more effectively, use plants in new ways to avoid or compensate for past mistakes. Since perennials are persistent and forgiving plants, we get not only second chances but innumerable chances. The continuity aspect of working with perennials, in terms of both their lifespan and the recurrence of opportunity, is irresistible.

Perennials are such a diverse and international group of plants. Although most are native to the Temperate Zone, which consists of those regions of the world that lie between Tropical and Arctic/Antarctic zones, there are vast differences in topography and climate within temperate areas. So there are tall and short plants suited to growing in a wide range of conditions, altitudes, and climates that are available and from which we can choose.

PLANTS ARE MULTINATIONAL

Plant explorers, since earliest times, have searched the world to find ornamental plants. Many early plant explorers came to America from Europe and the earliest was probably John Clayton, who arrived on our shores in 1705. Mark Catesby was another and Peter Kalm, who was from Sweden, took our mountain laurel (*Kalmia*) back to Europe. John Bartram, a Quaker from Philadelphia, was the first serious American botanist, and in 1780 he founded one of our first botanical gardens. The Philadelphia area became the center of gardening in North America; seeds and plants found by Bartram were regularly sent to Europe, and he also imported rare plants here from abroad. This is interesting because the Philadelphia Flower Show, considered by many to have the finest floral displays in the United States, continues to attract visitors each March, building on the city's horticultural traditions. Every flower lover should visit this flower show at least once in his or her lifetime.

While explorers and plant collectors do the fieldwork necessary for the globalization of plants, hybridists work on the plants to improve the specimens found in the wild and convert them into cultivated varieties. Every time we admire a lovely garden today we see the results of the work of talented plant breeders, and it was probably John Bartram who was the father of hybridization of garden flowers in our country. However, many others contributed to the introduction of plants that are now commonplace in gardens. Alexander Garden gave his name to the gardenia. Joel Poinsett, our first ambassador to Mexico and a native of Charleston, brought home poinsettias, and because of him we now have them in our homes for the holidays. Of course hybridizers were responsible for improving them, so that the greenhouse-grown plants we purchase are far different from the leggy specimens Poinsett found growing outdoors in the wild in Mexico. George Washington was also an accomplished plantsman, and his diaries and notes were used to restore his gardens at Mount Vernon, which can still be admired today. Thomas Jefferson introduced and grew many species of plants at Monticello and also wrote about horticultural methods. Toward the end of his life he said, "I am still devoted to the garden. But although I am an old man, I am still a young gardener."

From the time of the arrival of the early colonists, there was a deep interest in finding and developing ornamentals from abroad that would take root and thrive in the soil of the New World. Plants sent from the American colonies also injected new vigor into the gardens of Europe. English gardeners especially loved our native American fall-blooming asters. After their hybridizers improved them, Americans ceased to consider them roadside weeds and introduced them into their own gardens as prized perennials, welcoming them home like prodigal sons. From Europe came spring crocus (*Crocus vernus*) and snowdrops (*Galanthus nivalis*) as well as the taller snowflake (*Leucojum vernum*), and each spring they seem so at home when they bloom in our gardens that it is hard to believe that they weren't always here. Foxgloves (*Digitalis purpurea*) and sweet scabious (*Scabiosa atropurpurea*), commonly called pincushion flower, first grew in European gardens and had medicinal uses. Digitalis is well known as a heart remedy and the scabious was used to ameliorate itching of the skin.

Many scholars believe that the first plants grown for ornamental purposes, rather than for food, were grown near the Nile River. In ancient Egyptian gardens, judging from funeral wreaths found in tombs, flowers such as narcissus, cornflower, and lily appear to have been cultivated. In other Mediterranean cultures, many flowering bulbs were cultivated also, especially lilies, jonquils, and poet's narcissi. Grape hyacinth was native to and abundant in the Mediterranean region. Even the larger hyacinth that we now associate with the Dutch was probably native to areas near Greece and eastward into Asia.

Wars helped plants move around in ancient times, as soldiers took seeds and plants back home after fighting on foreign soil. For example, the Roman soldiers carried plants to distant parts of their empire (they took the snowdrop, *Galanthus nivalis*, to England) and also brought plants from far afield back to Rome. Around the European coast of the Mediterranean Sea, native plants such as the snapdragon (*Antirrhenum majus*) and candytuft (*Iberis*) grew robustly. The English common name of "snapdragon" is based on the way the two lips of the flower snap open when the side of the flower is pressed. Evidently children many years ago, like modern children, enjoyed this kind of floral game. Candytuft's common name derives from the fact that the plants grew well in Crete (Candia), and the botanical name is based on some species being native to Spain (Iberia).

Wild species of tulips were also native to the Mediterranean but it was in Turkey that they were first hybridized. The Austrian ambassador to the Sultan of Turkey sent them back to Vienna in 1554. The court gardener to

Maximilian II in Vienna later became a professor at the University of Leiden in Holland, so it was probably because of Professor Clusius that the tulip became popular in Holland. By the early 1630s "tulipomania" engulfed Holland as newly developed varieties were sold for huge amounts of money. This wild speculation eventually led to the solid industry in bulbs which is still an important part of the economy of the Netherlands today.

The Persians equated gardens with Paradise and were famous for their pleasure gardens. On ancient Persian rugs, some recognizable flowering plants can be seen, though rug-making later on used more geometric patterns. The Oriental poppy (*Papaver orientale*) and the crown imperial (*Fritillaria imperialis*) were native to Persia. Because scarcity of water was a problem throughout western Asia, flower garden plots were kept small. However, the Persians, like us, experimented with irrigation and also with combinations of plants so that there would always be something in bloom. So many gardeners, across so many centuries, have yearned for a progression of bloom. All flower gardeners, ancient and modern, have much in common, including the challenge of providing enough water for their ornamental plants.

South Africa was the original home of what we now call the red hot poker plant (*Kniphofia*, pronounced nee-FOE-fee-uh), but the hybridizers have improved this South African native a great deal. South Africa has played an important role in the development of ornamental plants and among that country's gifts to our gardens are the Calla Lily (*Zantedeschia*), which belongs to the *Arum* family, which also includes jack-in-the-pulpit. Impatiens, the best flowering annual for shade, is a native of East Africa, and the hybridizers have done wonders with it and provided us with a dazzling range of colors for our annual shade garden plantings. Other annuals from Africa include pelargoniums (we refer to them as the annual geraniums and often grow them in pots) and the tender gladiolus bulb. A favorite house plant, the African violet, also hails from Africa, as one would expect given its name.

Marco Polo was amazed when he first saw gardens in China. China is a vast country and has many climates and different types of soil, so China has provided many flowering plant species to the horticultural world and many Chinese natives grow exceptionally well in other countries in the Temperate Zone. Our much loved herbaceous peony (*Paeonia lactiflora*) has been cultivated in China for centuries. Two main types are grown: one is this well-known herbaceous peony, and the other is the tree peony, with a shrub-like habit that does not die down in winter. The sheen of the petals of the tree peony flowers is reminiscent of taffeta or silk, and a tree peony in bloom becomes a focal point in a garden. The poet Matsuo Basko must have been thinking of these shimmering flowers when he wrote, "A bee escapes from the heart of a peony with such regret." The magnificent regal lily (*Lilium regale*) as well as the hollyhock (*Althea rosea*), blackberry lily (*Belamcanda chinensis*), chrysanthemum, clematis, and forsythia all came to our gardens from China.

Many Chinese species came to us via Japan, which, with its variation in latitude, has a similar climate range to that of our Eastern seaboard from Florida to New England. A favorite bleeding heart in our perennial gardens, *Dicentra spectabilis*, is a Japanese native, although there are native American bleeding hearts too. Of course the Japanese iris is useful for extending the bloom period of irises in our gardens since it blooms later than the Siberian, Dutch, and German bearded types. The tall sword-like leaves of all iris plants also provide vertical height and the many varieties ensure a long series of bloom time in our gardens.

The hybridist and plant selector take natives, what many may call wild plants, and reconstitute them into improved versions of themselves. Sometimes, however, gardeners think hybridizers have gone too far in their efforts to improve on nature. Think, for example, as many remind us, of the hybrid tea roses that have been bred to look so perfect but have no perfume at all, and the dinner-plate-sized dahlias that can't hold up their heads in a vase. Generally speaking, hybridizers accomplish amazing feats for which all flower gardeners should be grateful. However, we sometimes would be well advised to wait a bit after the new selections are introduced, as they are usually more expensive initially than they are later on. It is also helpful to see how new cultivars do in other gardens in our own region, and to read about how they are rated by horticultural associations and magazines, before we try them. This kind of patience often pays off, and fortunately patience is a virtue one learns through gardening.

We gain many insights through gardening. As mentioned earlier, time is something that is inextricably woven into the fabric of gardening. So let us turn our attention once more to the construct of time, as it is an integral part of the development of both gardens and gardeners.

TIME IN THE GARDEN

For everyone, time is a limited commodity, so time in our gardens is precious, as it has to compete with many other compelling demands. However, it is rare for other activities to infuse us with the feeling that time stands still, the way it seems to do when we are immersed in our flower gardens. We step outside, intent on completing just one discrete task, and that task flows into another and yet another until, with a start, we realize we have been in the garden for hours.

Time loses its sharp edge when the tranquility of the garden claims us. It may be that at an unconscious level, our priorities shift. We don't even seem to articulate the thought, but it transpires nonetheless, that no chore awaiting indoors seems even remotely as important as those claiming our attention outside. Our level of satisfaction in the garden reorders our priorities. In the long run, of course, we understand, and assuage pangs of guilt by remembering, the enormous benefits to both our health and our dispositions. While gardening we learn to give ourselves time to receive intangible as well as tangible benefits.

Time-Sensitive Tasks

There are times, naturally, when other priorities must claim the attention of even the most devoted flower gardener. Fortunately, most flowering herbaceous perennials are forgiving. If we don't get supports in place at the right time, our tall plants will flop over but they won't die. If we don't deadhead meticulously on schedule, we will have fewer flowers, to be sure, but many perennials can be cut back hard later and some may throw a second flush of blooms. There are herbicides, such as Roundup, that can be used to spray out-of-control weeds if we neglect to pull them when they are small (use a piece of cardboard to shield neighboring plants from the spray). There is even a spray that will kill only the grass and not the perennials, if grass has invaded the beds. So, there is often a remedy when we miss a time-sensitive chore in the garden, and of course, with perennials, there is always next year.

The chore that really is time-sensitive is watering during prolonged drought. Always if possible make time to water plants that are stressed by lack of moisture. Wilting and yellowing and crisping of leaves should not be ignored. While a plant that wilts once or twice may be saved if the plant is deep watered, multiple wilts or prolonged wilting spells disaster. Deep watering once a week for established perennials and more frequent waterings for newly planted ones are necessary when there is a lack of rain.

GETTING TO KNOW PLANTS

Perennial plants have intriguing horticultural histories and the more we study them, both through reading and learning about them and by practicing growing them, the more responsive they seem to be to us. It is similar to the way friendships evolve and grow as we become more intimate with people. We gradually learn where they are from, their likes and dislikes, and special gifts we can give them that suit their personalities and needs. So it is with plants, and the process of understanding more about them enriches our interactions with them and our appreciation of them. Of course, as we get to know some perennials, we also have the option of dropping them from the lists of plants we grow if we find they don't like what we have to offer or if they are too finicky, or because they cause us too much work. Fortunately it is usually easier to eliminate high-maintenance plants from our gardens than it is to avoid difficult people. That said, we will now turn to ways we can choose to help our perennials become more satisfying for us. This involves adaptation on the part of the gardener as well as on the part of the plants.

We need to learn how to spot and respond to the signs that plants are struggling to adapt to both their site and the care they are receiving from us. Plants, as we have seen, have different requirements concerning sun and shade, the type of soil and level of nutrients, and the amount and regularity of watering. We have discussed earlier the importance of reading the plant labels so that we choose a site that is a good match for the needed amount of sun (and/or light in the case of shade plants).

Preferences concerning Moisture

We must be cognizant of the importance of good drainage, and how plants differ with respect to the way they can deal with soil that drains either too slowly or too quickly. Few plants are happy with constantly wet feet, and their leaves will turn yellow and their roots will rot if they are waterlogged for too long. This is because roots need air spaces in the soil in order for their little root hairs to remain viable. Plants that grow in pots must have drainage holes. Remember that porous clay pots dry out faster than plastic pots. Also small pots, containing less soil, always need more frequent watering than large pots. Plants in the ground have more soil from which roots can obtain moisture, but different species vary concerning how much sogginess they can tolerate. See appendix A for some perennials that will grow well in soil that doesn't drain well and is even bog-like.

Hot, dry slopes are also problematic, and if the soil lacks organic matter, which is what absorbs and holds the moisture, the problem is compounded. The solution is to find plants, usually those native to the Mediterranean, that love dry, well-drained soil. Many of these are grey-colored and/or have felted or hairy leaves which help retard evaporation of water. Many are aromatic (including thyme and lavender) and so are deer-resistant as well as drought-tolerant. Other drought-tolerant types of plants are succulents with fleshy, moisture-retentive leaves and roots (sedums, for instance). Sedums have both short and tall habits. The shorter-growing ones are useful in rock gardens and for edging, especially near concrete sidewalks and paths where conditions are too dry and hot for other short-statured perennials. The tall sedums add drama to the fall landscape. Perennials that are succulents and those with strong, broad root systems or tap roots (for example, prairie native wildflowers) are more equipped to shrug off drought. Always water perennials deeply, as frequent shallow watering only encourages shallow roots, which will make plants wilt quickly when drought comes. Deep-rooted plants survive dry conditions more easily. Learn to observe signs (such as wilting or drooping leaves) that signal that the plant is stressed by lack of moisture. Since sometimes yellowing leaves indicate too much instead of too little moisture, one needs to understand the difference. Also yellowing of leaves may sometimes occur as a result of certain nutrient deficiencies. In those cases the leaves will still be turgid, which indicates that lack of moisture is not the cause of the change in leaf coloration. See appendix B, "Drought- and Heat-Tolerant Perennials."

Varied Lifespans

The first year perennials are planted they usually do most of their expansion underground, getting their root systems established. All newly planted perennials need more regular watering at first than they will subsequently, to help them adjust to the site and settle in. In their second year they will begin to flower well. To earn the title of perennial, a plant must live for three or more years. Some, however, are extremely long-lived and may live many years. Peonies are reputed to live for one hundred years, though that claim is difficult to substantiate. Most soft-stemmed herbaceous perennials (as opposed to hard-stemmed shrubs) increase or self-sow, and so in one form or another persist in gardens for quite long periods once established. There are some, known as tender perennials, that are less reliable and may suddenly disappear and have to be replanted rather regularly if the gardener grieves at their demise and can't imagine a garden without them. These are sometimes biennials that we have mistaken for perennials. Biennials live only two years but frequently self-sow, and so may appear sometimes to be perennials.

Sub-shrubs

There are some perennial plants that are actually combinations of herbaceous plants and shrubs. These are known as sub-shrubs because they have a woody base like a shrub but their top growth is soft like that of an herbaceous perennial. It is easy to kill these types of plants (lavender, candytuft, and Russian sage, to name a few) if you cut them back too hard and injure the woody base. I used to cut back my lavender hard every fall, when I cut back all of my other perennials. The effects were disastrous and, complaining loudly, I had to buy new lavenders every spring. I had learned the drainage lesson well, and had them sited on a slope, but I hadn't realized they were sub-shrubs. It was my hacking away at the woody base that had murdered them. Now I wait to prune my lavender plants until late spring, or even into June, when it is easy to see what is the new, versus the old, growth. Then, and only then, do I snip off the old top growth very carefully. Thanks to a gardening friend who gave me an article on sub-shrubs, I now never, under any circumstances, cut into the woody base. This cautionary tale of my indiscretions with sub-shrubs should not deter you, however, from taking up your shears and deadheading spent blossoms on perennials.

Deadheading

Deadheading, the snipping of spent flowers to encourage new bloom, is an exemplary and highly necessary activity for all flower gardeners. Most perennials flower for two to three weeks at a preordained, very specific time of their growing season. Some bloom over a longer period, up to twelve weeks in some cases, and others can be encouraged to bloom again after their first flush (tall phlox and short cranesbills are two such plants). However, all must be deadheaded or they will set seed and put all of their energy into reproduction instead of into new blossoms. Flowers are the world's most efficient agents of self-perpetuation if allowed to go to seed. Cut a dead flower off just above the first leaf below that flower, but try to leave any buds that have formed above the leaves. Cut leafless flower stalks (such as bearded iris and day lilies) to the ground after all buds have opened and bloomed out. To encourage repeat bloom on bushy plants such as dianthus with lots of small flower heads, use shears to cut off all of the flowers, giving the entire plant the equivalent of a haircut. After they bloom, cut all varieties of cranesbill geranium and catmint back about two-thirds of the entire plant size. They will respond with new growth and more flowers later on.

Pinching

Early in the growing season, pinch out some plants' growing points by breaking or cutting the top of stems just above a pair of leaves further down. This keeps plants such as chrysanthemums from becoming lanky. Late-summer and fall bloomers, such as asters and boltonia, can be cut back by half once in the spring and again when the plants are 1½ feet tall. This will make them more compact and also promote additional flowers. You can also pinch off the side buds of flowers such as peonies to increase the size of the terminal flowers.

Be sure to disbud only when buds are really tiny, and don't worry about ants on peony buds as they are not a risk to the flowers. Just be sure you don't carry those ants into the house when you pick peonies. Shake the stems after you cut them to dislodge the little critters. Any time the foliage of perennial plants looks shabby after blooming, do not be afraid to cut it back to neaten up the garden. Cutting off the faded heads of plants such as tall garden phlox and also monarda will bring a second flush of flowers. There won't be as many, but there will be some.

Cutting Back

It is also possible to use cutting back as a method to slow down the timing of a perennial's period of bloom. If you are going to be on vacation during the time that a favorite plant regularly blooms, you can cut the plant back in order for it to bloom on a later schedule. Just remember that plants take approximately six weeks to set their buds and that it takes additional energy if they are cut back. So give them a little fertilizer to compensate them for their extra trouble and be sure to do the math correctly when you are calculating the weeks.

I should also warn you that the taller varieties of fall-blooming asters will still be tall, no matter how much you try to cut them back. However, they will be less tall than they would be otherwise. To have short perennial asters you need to plant only the cultivars that are short—for example, the New England aster 'Purple Dome' or 'Professor Kippenburg' (lavender). Goldenrod (no, it doesn't cause allergic reactions) and joe-pye weed, which combine well with tall asters, also benefit from cutting back early in the season to make them a little shorter in stature. Avant Gardens (www.avantgardensne.com), Wayside Gardens (www.waysidegardens.com), and Bluestone Perennials (www.bluestoneperennials.com) sell short-blooming asters as well as other excellent perennials.

VIGOR AND BALANCE

Perennials Don't Stand Still

Perennials bring variety into our gardens. There is the thrill of seeing their fresh green foliage return in the spring, as well as the pleasure of watching them grow and change throughout their growing season. They present a range of habits and shapes and sizes, and many have lovely foliage, which contributes to the overall feel and pattern of the garden. Try to make pleasing combinations of the tall and short, spindly and dumpy, airy and dense characteristics they offer, and plant, as Miss Jekyll advised, in threes and in drifts. Like people, plants have personalities, and some like to reproduce rapidly, crowding together, while others are more solitary. We all soon learn which ones are aggressive and which ones need coaxing along. In order to perfect the game of always having something in bloom, we all have to come to the realization that if we are too permissive we end up with too much of too few plants. For example, monarda will take over an entire bed in the blink of an eye. While it will be a glorious swathe of color in June if we let it have its way (remember, it is a member of the mint family), one type of plant is insufficient for a perennial parade. We have to be ruthless and yank out some of it so that there is room for other plants to bloom subsequently at their appointed times. I hate to pull out anything before it flowers, but unless we banish monarda to a playground of its own, it will engulf less vigorous plants unless it is thinned. Coexistence is not its strength, so our role is to ensure it stays only where we want it to be. Black-eyed Susans are vigorous spreaders too, so watch out for them, as well as yarrow and Japanese anemones. It is hard to have just a little of any of them, and yet they are necessary if we are to have color at their appointed times. Like unruly children some plants must be controlled, and we are the grown-up in our garden. Which brings us to the subject of division.

Division Is the Price of Success

When we start out we have too few perennials, and then before we know it we have too many. So we get out our spades and dig up the plants that have spread, because if they lose their vigor, bloom is compromised. Division rejuvenates our perennials and also prevents them from dominating small spaces by crowding other plants out. If we have large gardens, we can dig them up, divide them, and replant them to form drifts in the same location. Or we can make another new bed and transplant them. It is tempting to make new beds, but, even in the largest garden, this strategy is not one we can pursue indefinitely.

Timing, one of the most important aspects of gardening in all of its dimensions, is paramount with respect to dividing perennials. The rule is that plants take about a month to get their roots settled in. So we should replant divisions at least a month before they will be stressed by extremes of temperature. Ideally, they need to be settled into their new homes a month before it gets too unbearably hot in mid-summer or freezing cold in late autumn. Plants should not be moved when they are in flower. While we've all committed this sin, it is not in the plants' best interests. So, this leaves us a window in late spring to early summer to divide our spring bloomers, and one in early spring (when they have about 4" of top growth) to divide our summer and autumn bloomers. However, in areas with long and cool autumns where the killing frosts come late we can divide both spring and fall bloomers a month before freezing weather sets in. The longer the growing season is in your particular region, the longer you will have to divide and transplant each fall. Gardening in a zone where there are long falls is a true bonus, as there is time to divide and replant while cool conditions prevail.

A sharp knife can be used to cut the woody roots of plants such as *Astilbe* or bleeding heart, and the sections can then be replanted at the same depth at which they were originally growing. Peonies must be planted no deeper than 1 to 1½ inches below the surface or the new divisions will never flower. Try to ensure that there are about three eyes (or buds) on each woody rootstock. Clumped roots of non-tuberous plants can be separated by driving a spade or two forks into the middle of the clump, and hostas can be dug up entirely and cut into sections, or sections may be spaded out from the sides of the plants. Though it takes some courage to start dividing our precious and robust-looking plants, once we examine the root systems or rhizomes we can see where the growing points are and identify how the rhizomes can be separated so that enough remains to sustain new growth. Trial and error is a good way to learn, and there are usually enough divisions available from mature root systems that if we plant enough some will grow. We can stick a few in pots as insurance, too.

Replanting

Choose a cool, cloudy day to plant and "mud in" the divisions by soaking the area around them with water so that there are no big air pockets between the roots and the soil. Water the new plants each day to help them get established. After they are established, one inch of water per week is usually enough, depending of course on rainfall and the type and sites of plantings.

It is always best to water using a method that avoids drenching the foliage if possible (soaker hoses or water from a can directed onto the roots are two good methods). Overhead watering encourages mildew and other unfortunate diseases. While I am on the subject of planting (container plants that have been purchased as well as divisions that have remained in pots for a while), we should always dig a hole twice as wide and deep as the root system of the plant and spread the roots out or down according to the type of roots. Place the soil under as well as over the roots. Add some compost or leaves to help amend the soil while you are at it. Mix in some fertilizer also.

Compacted Roots

If the roots are compacted in a pot and appear to be circling the root ball, use a knife or claw to cut the root ball from top to bottom. This will help roots to grow outwards. Cut into the root ball to stimulate new growth. You can even cut ½ to 1 inch off the bottom of the root ball. Established container plants can be planted after they are purchased or when they have enough roots in the pots to make the transfer into the ground without much trauma. Since they have not had complete transplant surgery, their transition will be less challenging than that of fresh divisions, though they will still need one month's grace before the temperatures go to freezing.

Bare Roots

Bare-root plants that are shipped will arrive at the appropriate time for planting in your region. Keep them moist and in a dark spot and don't expose roots to sun or wind before they are covered with earth in the ground. Place them upwards (the main stalk or new shoots will mark the crown or growing point) and separate the roots so they go either out or down according to their habit. Mud them in well and water regularly until they take off. If the weather is not cool or cloudy, cover them with a basket or large pot for a few days after planting to shade them.

Staking Plants

Timing is also important with respect to when and how plants are staked. If metal grow rings are to be used they should be placed over the plant early, before much above-ground growth has occurred. Any prongs from the wire rings, wire cages, or stakes that are used to provide support are best inserted into the ground near the plant before the plant grows too large and the root system expands. It is tough to wrestle with putting a wire frame over a tall plant, so it should be in place before the stems grow too high. Oriental lilies and other tall plants with heavy blossoms always benefit from strong stakes that prevent them from being blown over during summer storms. Use sections of nylon pantyhose to tie stems to stakes, or other ties that do not cut into the stems and damage them.

DESIGN AND COLOR

Visit Other Gardens

Seeing a variety of other private gardens, as well as public gardens, is often more instructive than merely reading about garden design. We know what we like when we see it and experience it for ourselves. So if there are garden tours in your area or garden trips that are arranged by garden clubs or tour groups, take the opportunity to see other peoples' gardens. Take a notebook to record names of plants you like and other ideas you could use. Notice the colors you like and the color combinations that appeal to you. Do you respond to cool pastel shades, or do you like warm strong colors? What style of garden appeals to you most? Do you like cottage gardens? Or are you drawn to naturalistic meadow plantings? Is the sound of water important to you in a garden or do you long for plants that attract songbirds and butterflies?

After visiting other gardens, check out some books on garden design from the library and try to determine your preferred garden style. Also make a list of garden functions you desire—for example, a place to sit outside, outdoor entertainment areas, a play area for children, visual appeal from the street, privacy screens, and so forth.

Hardscape

Hardscape is the term given to non-plant items in the garden, including walls, paths, trellises, arbors, decks, patios, raised beds, and so on. Again, visiting other gardens increases awareness about options with respect to the designs and types of materials that are available. Books and magazines are also good sources of ideas, and some will provide instructions for building various items.

Color

Color is important in flower gardens, of course. While beautiful and serene gardens can be made using various shades of foliage, deciding on the palette you prefer for your flowers is important in promoting an overall color scheme that is coherent. First decide if you are drawn to strong, bold colors or to delicate pastel hues. Consider whether warm hues or cool hues attract your attention. Once you have decided on the category, think of about five complementary colors that you like. By zeroing in on color combination, you then will find it easy to select plants with colors within your group and to ensure that all your selections combine well in the garden. One such group might be pink, pinkish reds, blues, purples, and whites. Touches of lemon yellow could also be used as accents in the above grouping. Another grouping could include orange, orangey reds, strong yellows, purples, and blues, with whites as accents. There are many groupings that will work depending on what appeals to you personally.

The next step is to try to find something in your preferred color palette that blooms at each point in the growing season. Since the colors should all work together, overlapping of flowers when they are blooming will not be a problem. You should also have both short and tall plants represented in your selections, and hopefully some flowers with spikes and some with mounded flower heads. Foliage contrasts will also be helpful to the overall design. A pastel garden will benefit from some grey foliage, as Miss Jekyll taught us, and strong colors will look even better with dark foliage accents, as Christopher Lloyd (1921–2006) demonstrated so well in his garden at Great Dixter in England. Chartreuse foliage is also an excellent foil for many colors, especially purple and white and blue. See appendix C for grey foliage plants and appendix D for dark foliage plants.

As Alexander Pope said, "All gardening is landscape painting." We will now move to the discussion of what blooms when—that is, the spring, summer, and autumn bloomers that will ensure that you plant a succession of perennials to provide your preferred colors across the growing season.

THREE

Flowers across Three Seasons

Spring is exuberant
with promise.
Summer is lavish
with abundance.
Autumn is mellow,
yet bittersweet.

It is convenient to categorize the plants according to their seasons of bloom, though of course all herbaceous perennials (but not the bulbs) contribute foliage that creates the tapestry of our gardens in each of the three growing seasons.

So, in this chapter we will be considering flowering perennials that also have diverse growth patterns and attractive foliage. All characteristics of plants are important in garden design as flowering ebbs and flows. It takes some years to have complete continuity of bloom, and even an established perennial garden with a back-up of flowering shrubs, vines, and trees will sometimes have blank spots. Deer may be the culprits, but there are other innumerable possibilities for disasters that can occur. Of course, the larger the garden, the more insurance we have against times without any perennial in bloom. References such as lists of plants help us add more than one type of plant per timeframe to carry the show outside and to fill our vases inside. So there are lists in the appendices to provide a guide for choices of both short and tall growers, according to the times they bloom and the conditions they prefer.

SPRING

First a howling blizzard woke us
Then the rain came down to soak us
And now before the eye can focus—
CROCUS.

—*Lilja Rogers*

This is an exciting time for gardeners, fuelled by ardent anticipation of seeing their plants coming to life again as winter releases its iron grip on the earth. However, there can be disappointments also in the spring, when alternate freezing and thawing may damage new growth. The tiny bulbs appear first, and we can never have too many of these tough little miracles. Winter aconite, with tiny yellow cup-shaped flowers, the milky white snowdrops, and the delicate lavender early crocus lead the parade, and they are at their best when we see them naturalized in older gardens. They remind us that some gardener planted probably only a few tiny bulbs one autumn day long ago. These miniature flowers perform each year for only a fleeting time, but the recurrence and continuity of their display creates an awesome legacy. If you are lucky enough to be able to get a start of winter aconite from an established planting, your chances of getting them to naturalize will be enhanced. Dig them with clumps of earth attached while they are in bloom, before they disappear. While the aconites are the first to bloom, they are soon followed by lots of other short early bloomers. Some of these are listed in appendix E.

> Fair-handed spring unbosoms every grace—
> throws out the crocus and the snowdrop first
>
> —*James Thomson*

The advantage of planting small bulbs is that one does not have to dig deep holes in the fall. It is easy to scoop out a one-foot wide, four-inch deep hole and arrange lots of little bulbs in it. Since there will be autumn leaves lying around as you are digging, throw a handful of those into each hole, as this is a simple way of increasing the organic matter in the soil. Remember also to put some fertilizer into each hole, preferably a granular or other type with no odor. Strong-smelling fertilizers invite rodents to investigate what has been buried.

Larger Bulbs

> And then my heart with pleasure fills
> and dances with the daffodils
>
> —*William Wordsworth*

Although we cannot ever have enough drifts of small-bulb flowers, we need to plant large bulbs each fall, too, in order to keep our spring procession of flowers going after the miniatures have finished. So it is essential to plant daffodils, for example, that represent early-, mid-, and late-season bloomers. Daffodils belong to the genus *Narcissus*, and technically a daffodil is a narcissus with a trumpet that is as long as or longer than the surrounding petals. Sometimes the trumpet is a different color from the petals, but there is always just one flower on each stem. There are also types of narcissus (e.g., *N. jonquila*) that have shallow cups. Jonquils bloom later than the large single narcissi with trumpets, and they have shallow cups and clusters of flowers on one stem; they are more fragrant than other narcissi. There is also another type of narcissus, a late bloomer called the pheasant eye or poet's narcissus, which makes a lovely accent in the garden; the delicate edging on its shallow cup is seen to advantage in a vase. All members of this family are deer-resistant and persist, and even increase, from year to year. So if you want a large planting of spring bulbs, the many varieties of *Narcissus* are the ones to choose. Tulips are unfortunately beloved by deer, and also the tall stately ones usually do not behave like perennials. If you plant the early short-stemmed tulips (such as *T. kaufmanniana*) you will have better luck, however, as long as Bambi is not around.

> With excellent precision
> the tulip bed
> inside an iron fence
> upreared its gaudy
> yellow, white and red,
> rimmed round with grass,
> reposedly.
> —*William Carlos Williams*

Although bulbs (see appendix F) provide us with some of the most well-loved and showy spring flowers, other perennials are useful during the spring season and combine well with bulbs. Since bulbs need to make food for the next year, their foliage, which is essential for this process, must be allowed to die down naturally. Creeping and mounded perennials can provide not only a foil for the bulbs but also camouflage for the foliage once the blooms are spent.

Short Herbaceous Perennials

> How could such sweet and wholesome hours
> Be reckoned without herbs and flowers?
> —*Andrew Marvel*

The list in appendix G includes some small plants that are short-lived perennials (such as *Viola tricolor*, Johnny-jump-up, which is included because it self-sows and has such a charming little face). Some others on the list are invasive in a small bed but wonderful ground covers in woodland gardens. Since there are sometimes places in our gardens where we want plants that spread, these plants (snow-in-summer, aggressive bellflower, bluets, and *Corydalis lutea* [yellow], *Epimedium* and *Lamium* [good in dry shade], and *Ajuga* and *Vinca* [ground covers]) have been listed. However, gardeners should be wary about placing such plants in small beds, where the spreaders can become unruly. Always read the plant tags carefully and seek advice from other gardeners, and do not be afraid to dig up plants that are too vigorous for a site before they become a long-term nuisance. Spring is also the season to start weeding, as small weeds are the easiest to dislodge and haven't set seeds.

> Now 'tis spring, and weeds are shallow rooted;
> Suffer them now and they'll o'ergrow the garden.
> —*William Shakespeare, King Henry VI, 1592*

Taller Herbaceous Perennials

Tall perennials (see appendix H) add vertical interest to a garden and contrast with the shorter specimens. Taller plants are usually placed at the back of a border or in the middle of a bed. Or they can be placed together in front of a shrub or used alone as an exclamation point at the end of a bed or by a doorway. Plants that don't look right in one spot can always be moved. Trial and error is a time-honored strategy of all gardeners and most of us are usually moving something around in our gardens. It is what we do.

Spring is a season in which our beds and borders are often enhanced by the flowering trees and shrubs in our own or neighboring yards. Also, professional designers tell us that one-third of garden plantings should be evergreens to provide structure during all four seasons of the year. In the spring, when our early flowers bloom but there is not yet a great deal of herbaceous foliage, evergreens also provide an important backdrop and create a dark contrast for spring bloomers. Forsythia is a deciduous shrub that is useful in the spring display, but it needs to be given a place of its own, as forsythia is an unruly fellow and will quickly take over. Although glorious when in bloom, it is not an especially attractive shrub once its moment of glory is past. Use forsythia as hedges or specimens in places where they are out of the way of your perennials. Karl Capek wrote knowingly, "Tomorrow the twigs of forsythia will be sprinkled all over the golden stars. You simply cannot hold it back." Fortunately, there are many other spring-blooming shrubs, and most of them are better-behaved than forsythia. All should be pruned only just after they have bloomed.

SUMMER

Our summer made her light escape
into the garden.

—Emily Dickinson

Early summer is a wonderful time in the garden. It is invigorating to be outside as everything is still fresh and green and many flowers come into bloom. This is when many garden tours are organized, since roses and daylilies are blooming and so many other plants are at their best. Summer gives us, and the plants too, perhaps, a rush of adrenaline.

If we are wise we make sure our gardens are weeded and mulched. Mulch inhibits weeds and prevents the soil from drying out. It also makes a flower bed or border look neat and organized. Mulch does for plants what black velvet does for a piece of jewelry; it is the background of choice.

Focal Points

While thinking of jewelry I am reminded that George Croly wrote that "flowers are nature's jewels with whose wealth she decks her summer beauty." However, foliage and inanimate decorative items can also serve in the roles of garden gems. Tom Hobbs, a nurseryman and designer in Vancouver, British Columbia, advocates what he calls "jewel box" vignettes in gardens. He combines plants in delicious colors and shapes and often adds an object such as a luminous glass globe or some interesting colored stones to pick up the color or contrast with foliage. It is an interesting extension of the concept of focal points in gardens and one that is thought-provoking in terms of its applications. Sometimes we want to redirect attention from an aspect of our garden that is, either permanently or temporarily, not up to par. We can place a grouping of plants nearby, even perhaps in pots, to be an attention-grabber, so that all eyes turn to something that is beautiful. Or we can use the element of surprise and tuck an exquisite combination of plants into an overlooked corner of the garden that garden visitors come upon unexpectedly. Even unabashed flower addicts need to think about the ways interesting foliage can be used and combined to optimize effects in perennial gardens. And remember, although we may be perennial gardeners to the core, it is not forbidden to have a few annual flowers or leafy wonder plants such as coleus to move around the garden, in pots, to places where they can provide a needed boost. Succulents in pots are also useful, since they can be combined in interesting ways and don't need a lot of water. Try planting a selection of different-colored sedums in a wide, dish-shaped container for a relatively maintenance-free container accent.

Short and Tall Perennials

Set here the phlox and the iris, and establish
Pink and valerian, and the great and lesser bells.

—*Edna St. Vincent Millay*

Lists are provided in appendices I, J, and K to furnish ideas for many summer bloomers with differing bloom heads (bells, flat umbels, spires, clusters, etc.) as well as varied foliage. Use the list to play the marvelous garden game of mix and match, in terms of color and form, as well as to ensure that you have lots in bloom across the whole summer. Remember also to repeat some plants with pleasing shapes and/or colors. Repetition is an excellent strategy that helps to integrate plantings into coherent patterns. Edging beds and borders with the same kind of short plants also provides organization in a garden. Alternating two types of plants or the same plant with two different colors of bloom is also an interesting technique.

Clematis and Roses

Of course there are exceptional flowering vines (clematis, for example) that enable us to have vertical highlights in our gardens even though it is the herbaceous perennials that we are focusing on in this book. Also, most of us long for roses, and some, such as the ones with "Knock Out" in their names, are disease-resistant and do not need deadheading. Polyantha shrub roses such as 'The Fairy' and the All-American Rose Selection 'Bonica' also bear clusters of pink flowers in flushes all through the summer. Climbing roses such as 'New Dawn' and 'Zepherine Drouhin' also do well in my own Midwest garden. Climbers are difficult when winters are very cold and/or the growing season is short. This is because the plants don't have enough time to put out sufficient new growth to adequately cover their supporting structure before they die back to the ground each winter.

Renegade Perennials

In my long list of summer perennials you will not find gooseneck loosestrife (*Lysimachia clethroides*) or yellow circle flower (*Lysimachia punctata*). Nor will you find purple loosestrife (*Lythrum salicaria*), which crowds out native plants. These vigorous spreaders are prolific bloomers but I think that all three are just too aggressive to be included, even though I admire their flowers. Purple loosestrife is actually classified as an invasive plant in North America. Invasive plants escape from gardens, invade the ecosystem, and alter its structure. This is dangerous to our native plants because they are choked out. We should not give any invasive plant a place in our garden, as we want to be good stewards of the earth. Aggressive plants such as the other two mentioned above and our native monarda, while they spread and must be controlled in the garden, are not dangerous to our ecosystem.

GARDEN STYLES

Some people like to make of life a garden,
and to walk only within its paths.

—*Japanese proverb*

Paths

When designing a new garden, it is often helpful to first plan where the paths might go, since paths help to define garden spaces. Paths can be curved or straight, but they should allow both the gardener and visitors to navigate the garden easily. If you have a large tree in your yard, you may consider installing a bench underneath its shade, with a path that leads to it. Or you may decide to plant a shade garden of woodland-type plants encircling it. In the latter instance you might install a path of stepping stones through the woodland garden. Always have a path leading to your door from the street or driveway that has a safe surface and is preferably wide enough for two people to walk side by side. Paths in other parts of the garden can be narrower but you may wish to make them wide enough for the wheelbarrow or mower to traverse easily. If you make paths through lawn areas, install an edging that makes mowing efficient and prevents grass from invading flower beds. Paths define the garden and allow for slow walks through various areas. Bends in paths can provide opportunities to plant shrubs or tall perennials to screen views until visitors round the bend. Think carefully about how the layout of your paths can create a pleasing overall effect and help showcase your perennial plantings.

Generalizations about Styles

The more formal the garden, the more well-behaved the plants need to be. Formal gardens usually have well-defined perimeters, manicured evergreens, urns, and straight and orderly brick or stone paths that bisect the plantings.

Japanese-style gardens are formal, and they have serene spaces that rely not on flowers, but on varied green textures and carefully placed pebbles and stone. Mediterranean gardens have romantic courtyards. American gardens, once strongly influenced only by English gardens with exuberant curving floral borders and cottage-style flower beds, now are reflecting more varied influences. For example, Xeriscaping, which is a response to the need to be conservative with respect to use of water, has resulted in more naturalistic designs using drought-tolerant plants. In the more informal modern American gardens, plants lean against their neighbors, and native plants and grasses (ones that don't aggressively self-sow) are emphasized. Woodland gardens, capitalizing on wildflowers and shade-loving perennials, have also gained in popularity. Gardening is the most popular hobby in the United States, and the hybridizers are so busy nowadays that garden catalogs and nurseries are brimming with new introductions. Modern plant explorers, too, including Dan Hinkley, have brought to our attention many new plants from abroad that can also be grown in the United States. There are so many selections to consider that we may sometimes feel overwhelmed. However, it is a very stimulating time to be a gardener and to have access to so many beautiful plants. One of the most well-known amateur gardeners of all time, Vita Sackville-West, wrote, "The secret of good gardening: Choose always the best of any variety you want to grow."

Globe-Trotting Plants

As noted earlier, globalization is not a new trend in horticulture because plants have always been world travelers. The ancient mariners carried seeds on their sailing ships. Some seeds were even stowaways in the ballast of ships and grew where the ballast was unloaded on distant shores. Wherever explorers went in times past, they found new plants to take back to their homelands. Some, such as Captain Cook, even had a botanist on board, and Sir Joseph Banks described, drew, and took samples home to England of the plants found during Cook's voyages around the Pacific and to Australia and New Zealand in the 1700s.

The ubiquitous chrysanthemum is an example of a globe-trotting plant that has traveled far since it set out from its original home in China. For those of us living in the Northern Hemisphere it blooms during the months of August, September, and October. In the Southern Hemisphere it blooms for Mother's Day in many countries, since May is an autumn month in that part of the world. So we can nowadays buy chrysanthemums imported from South America in our spring, grown in their fall. And of course these serviceable flowers are grown everywhere in greenhouses, as they now are the quintessential flower for floral arrangements year-round. But we cannot think about chrysanthemums in this part of the world without thinking of fall gardens.

AUTUMN

September sunshine . . .
the hovering dragonfly's
Simmering shadow.

—Karo

The light changes in our gardens and the days grow shorter in the fall of the year and the play of shadow and light seems to intensify the depth of the colors of this season's flowers. Gardeners find new energy. This is probably not only because the air is cool and crisp, but because they have more urgency of purpose as the year wanes. Plants' growth slows, and there are other signs too of their impending mortality. Robert Penn Warren described the transitional nature of this season in the following lines:

Now poised between the two alarms
Of summer's lusts and winter's harms . . .

Transitions of all kinds are known for creating uneasiness at best and anxiety at worst, and gardeners are not exempt from these reactions as they sense that another growing season is about to end. However, autumn also is a satisfying season for flower gardeners.

For instance, those gardeners who plant with the aim of attracting birds, bees, and butterflies to their gardens are especially pleased by the activity around their flowers in autumn. Birds find colorful berries, the bees and butterflies are busy, and the vibrant air appears to hum.

And at times to hear the drowsy tones
of dizzy flies, and humming drones . . .

—Robert Bridges

It is convenient for the birds and insects that many fall bloomers have flat, wide flower heads. Sedums have rich textured heads that darken in the fall, and some large sunflowers may linger in the garden too. Bridges also wrote about them:

Where tomtits, hanging from the drooping heads
Of giant sunflowers, peck the nutty seeds . . .

The autumn garden is characterized by a rich mix of textures and by the harvesting of seeds, nectar, and berries by energetic birds and insects. The squirrels are usually out and about also. But they will collect not only nuts, but also our bulbs if we are not careful.

Short and Tall Perennials

It is impossible for us to imagine a perennial garden without chrysanthemums. However, as we plan our autumn sequence of bloom, we should also consider some of the other perennials that can be relied upon to carry our gardens through to the end of each year's growing season (see appendix L, "Fall-Flowering Perennials and Bulbs"). Asters, goldenrod, joe-pye weed, Japanese anemone, boltonia, sedum, Russian sage, and all of the various chrysanthemums as well as late-blooming daylilies, repeat-blooming bearded iris, and malva (which can be cut back earlier to encourage continued bloom) are vibrant at this time of the year. The shorter length of the days and the change in the light itself seem to make the colors of many fall bloomers even more intense.

Autumn brings such perfect weather to work in our gardens, and as we cut down the spent flower stalks and foliage we muse about all the flowers that we enjoyed over the summer and think of things we will do differently next year. It is a bittersweet time as we put our gardens to bed and do fall clean-up. But there are bulbs to plant, too, and that assures us of the promise hidden within each bulb, of flowers next spring. The papery jackets of the bulbs, the vibrant colors of the autumn leaves, and the clear blue of the sky are pleasures to savor. In the fall our procession of flowers is winding down for another year, but in the eternal rhythm of the seasons it will start up again next spring, and all we must do is be patient. So it is and always will be, that our garden is the metaphor that marks the seasons in our lives. The next few lines, also by Robert Bridges, describe how busy and beautiful the bees and the butterflies are in our fall flower gardens. The name *Aster* means "stars," and no fall garden should be without these beautiful clusters of small starry flowers.

> And in the feathery aster bees on wing
> Seize and set free the honied flowers,
> Till thousand stars leap with their visiting:
> While ever across the path mazily flit,
> Unpiloted in the sun,
> The dreamy butterflies
> With dazzling colours powdered and soft glooms,

White, black and crimson stripes, and peacock eyes,
Or on chance flowers sit,
With idle effort plundering one by one
The nectaries of deepest-threaded blooms.

—from "The Garden in September"

The mellow full-bodied flowers of autumn provide a grand finale to our progression of bloom across the three growing seasons. Even after the killing frosts come, the memories linger, while the roots of our perennials sleep, just waiting to be resurrected when spring comes again. As Marcel Proust wrote: "A change in the weather is sufficient to recreate the world and ourselves."

LEARNING FROM OUR GARDENS

This moral it is mine to sing
Go learn a lesson of the flowers

—Hafiz

Flower gardening teaches many lessons. Just as balance is a lesson to be learned in life, so it is in gardening. For instance, we learn to appreciate balance in terms of both control and serendipity. Flowering perennials need the gardener to exhibit control or certain plants will exceed their bounds, the garden's design will be blurred, weeds will take over, and so on. And yet too much control prevents the joys that result from serendipity. A plant pops up in an unexpected place and the result may be an effect that we would not have imagined, had we yanked it out too soon. Nature presents us with the benefits of unexpected bonuses in the garden if we relax our control, either by accident or design. This happens frequently in my garden when the big, tall *Nicotiana sylvestris* self-sows and pops up in odd places. If I let some of these new plants have their way, I am usually delighted with the result. Their fresh lettuce-green tobacco-type leaves and bell-shaped white flowers glow in the early evening and perfume the air. I would have considered them to be too tall for the spots they chose, but actually they look like lovely exclamation points when they take root and claim spaces of their own.

Another lesson I have learned from my flowering perennials is not to expect that plants, or indeed people, are all good or all bad. No plant fulfils all of our expectations. The issue really is, do the good points compensate for the bad? In any organization an administrator has to weigh what an individual member can contribute to the common good versus that person's few, but inevitable, negative characteristics. For example, creeping phlox (*Phlox subulata*) is glorious when it blooms in the spring but is quietly green for the rest of the growing season. It takes up space. Is its season of bloom sufficiently important to justify its long down-time? My answer is a resounding yes. I can't wait to see these phlox bloom in the spring. Their vivid colors, for even a short time, more than compensate for their down-time. High impact, even though it is relatively short, earns it a place in my garden. It pays its freight. This is just one example of the kinds of choices we learn to make as administrators of our gardens. We learn about making choices based on the overall context, applying our individualized, intensely personal cost/benefit formula.

Windows of Time

As was mentioned earlier, we learn a lot about time in our gardens, too. Time in our gardens is like a moment gone: For everything there is a season, and time waits for no man (or woman). Timing is especially crucial with respect to seed heads. Even if the gardener is busy with other things, flowers as well as weeds must not be allowed to set seeds unless you want to encourage self-sowing. In that case, scrape away the mulch around the plant. Mulch contains a seed germination deterrent to stop weed seeds germinating. Plants stop flowering when they set seeds, so snip them off promptly. Above all, get rid of those weeds before they set seed or you will have a new generation of weeds, even more prolific, with which to deal. There is a small window of time for deadheading, and that is that. Miss the opportunity and you will rue it. This is also the case with some other chores in the garden. There is a specific time to plant bulbs, a specific time to pinch plants back, set stakes and other supports in place, and water. To miss these times is to miss opportunities that, once passed, cannot be regained. Gardening teaches us the valuable lessons of discipline with respect to time. Plants are time-sensitive and flower gardeners must be aware of and respectful of time constraints and respond during those crucial windows of opportunity. So observe your plants carefully and respond to them at their required times. However, as we discussed earlier, sometimes we can't do what needs to be done at a specific time. When this happens we come to understand delayed gratification, and we let the disappointment go and move on. We look ahead to next year.

Time and Place

Time and place are both crucial considerations in the perennial flower garden. Understand the plant's background by identifying its place of origin, and site it in your garden with this in mind. Watch your flowering perennials so that you can respond to their needs and try to be there for them at the times that they need your attention. The perennial gardener doesn't need to be a slave to the garden, but does need to be responsive to the cycles in the lives of the plants. Perennials are not demanding plants, but there are times when they need their gardener to be there for them. After all, no matter where they come from originally, they have become part of our family, and like all family members, they flourish best when they get the attention they deserve. However, a little benign neglect from time to time is okay too.

Most gardeners know other gardeners and trade plants and ideas, enjoying the special bond forged by a common interest. So when we need to be away from our gardens, we are often blessed with a neighbor or friend who gardens and who will be happy to water or at least check on our gardens while we are out of town. We, of course, return the favor when they are absent. This kind of reciprocity is often preferable to hiring someone who doesn't share a deep interest in plants. Just as pleasing combinations of plants enhance each other, so do members of one's garden fraternity. Perhaps Martha Smith was thinking about this when she wrote: "Gardening is a habit of which I hope never to be cured, one shared with an array of fascinating people who helped me grow and bloom among my flowers."

FOUR

Displaying Flowers

A house with daffodils in it
is a house lit up,
Whether or not the sun
be shining outside.
Daffodils in a green bowl—
and let it snow if it will.

—*A. A. Milne*

ne of the benefits of growing perennials is the continual supply of cut flowers for the home and for sharing with neighbors and friends. Flowers, ideally already arranged in a container, are a hostess gift that is usually welcome. The busy hostess does not have to worry about finding a vase, cutting the stems, and putting them in water. Hopefully, the water will never spill in your car en route. If you transport a lot of flowers, keep a few bricks in your car to pack around flower containers. Small containers sometimes can be anchored in cup-holders, if your car has them, or in small cardboard boxes with crushed-up newspaper packed around them. Some passengers in cars will even willingly hold a vase full of flowers en route to an event. Should you be lucky enough to persuade a passenger in your car to cooperate in this way, be sure to put only a small amount of water in the flower container before you hand it over. Seat the person first, of course, and then place the vase either between the passenger's feet on the floor, or into the person's hands. I may be belaboring this point a bit here, but caution is important, for if a passenger arrives with wet clothes it is embarrassing to say the least.

START SMALL

If you lack either confidence or experience in arranging flowers, collect small bottles and vases and play with grouping a variety of flowers and foliage of different colors and textures. If you have limited amounts of plant material, choose containers with narrow or somewhat nipped-in necks so that even these few stems are supported and remain upright. With wide-necked containers, use a lot of flowers so they can support each other, or first pack some floral foam (Oasis) into the container. The stems can then be inserted into the wet foam so that they can be positioned more precisely. Experimentation is the best way for a novice to learn how to make pleasing arrangements. Cut the stems to different lengths and remember that usually an arrangement should be no taller than about one and a half times the height of the vase. If it is higher than this it will look top-heavy. Don't jam too many flowers into a container so that they obscure each other, but give them some breathing space.

TYPES OF ARRANGEMENTS

Arrangements can be made to stand against a wall or other backdrop, and arrangements like these are called "facing" arrangements. They are seen just from the front and sides, so we don't have to worry about the back view as it is never seen. Those types of arrangements can be of any height. If the flowers are to be placed on a table, however, the arrangement needs to be lower and either round or long and narrow. Centerpieces for dining tables, for example, must be low enough so that guests can see over them as they converse with others across the table. Use a low container and first soak Oasis for a while (preferably at least an hour) to ensure that it is completely waterlogged. A block of Oasis (available at hobby stores) that is bobbing on the top of the water in the sink or bucket in which it is soaking has not absorbed enough water. When it has sunk to the bottom, it is ready to use. Cut the block to fit snugly into and fill the container. If there are gaps, pack extra pieces of Oasis into them so that the whole container is full. For a round arrangement, cut all of the stems the same length and insert the stems of the foliage or filler into the Oasis first, until the Oasis is hidden from view. Then insert the flowers. For a dome shape, cut the stems to be inserted in the middle slightly longer than those used around the perimeter. For an elongated centerpiece shape, stick longer-stemmed flowers and foliage straight out horizontally into both ends of the Oasis so that they point their heads toward each end of the table.

Filler is the name given to foliage or frothy flowers (such as baby's breath or lady's mantle) that fill up the container, hide the underpinnings, and allow a smaller number of other flowers to be used. Foliage used in this way gives a lush green foil for the blooms, and baby's breath and other airy-type flower heads provide a softening effect. During the holiday season, evergreen foliage can be used this way, and holly-type leaves (preferably non-prickly varieties) can provide a glossy contrast for small red carnations nestled among them. Try to plant some evergreen shrubs in your yard that have good winter foliage so that you can dash out any time during the colder months and pick some. This enables you to cut down on the number of flowers you need to buy to nestle among the leaves. Carnations and mums are excellent for arrangements as they are long-lasting, come in a variety of colors, and have strong stems that insert easily into Oasis or pin-holders. If you use flowers or foliage with weak stems you must use a pencil or a skewer to make the hole in the Oasis before inserting the stem. Any device used to anchor flowers in a container (some have holes and some have spikes) is called a frog, because they sit in water. Look for glass or ceramic frogs in antique stores.

Triangular shapes are popular for flowers arranged in taller containers, especially facing arrangements (those viewed only from the front). Pack the vase with Oasis as the first step. Then place the taller flowers in the middle and toward the back and build the triangle by gradually reducing the height of the stems that you place at the sides. Fill in the middle of the arrangement with flowers and cut some stems smaller and angle the flower heads in front and at the sides to curve both out and down and obscure the container's rim: a fan-shaped display is a variation of this. In order to get the curve to be symmetrical on both sides of the highest middle point, cut two identical flowers to the exact same height and place one on each side of the center. Do this repeatedly, making the stems incrementally shorter as you move out from the center focal point. Once the outline is in place, the body of the arrangement can be filled in. Again, always angle some flowers forward to avoid a flat look.

CONDITIONING FLOWERS

Different flowers have different vase lives. However, there are some ways to prolong vase life. Plunge flowers into deep water and let them get a good drink as soon as they are picked or carried home from a store. Recut the stems under water before letting them soak up the water while standing in a container of water in a dark cool spot, preferably overnight. Strip off all leaves that will end up below the waterline before you place flowers in an arrangement. If you cut flowers from your own garden, do it after the sun goes down, conditioning them overnight so that they can adjust to their new circumstances, and you will have more success with the arrangement lasting well. Whether you buy flowers or pick your own, always choose the ones that are not yet fully developed unless it is just for one immediate occasion that you need them to be at their best. Daffodils should be closed but showing color or, if open, should still have fresh petal substance. Once the petals look papery they are on the wane. Roses and tulips should be still in bud. Only two or three of the lowest gladioli flowers should be open, and carnations should not be showing their white stamens in the center. Iris should also be in bud, and the flowers that die in an arrangement should always be pinched off so that successive buds will open. In order to prevent tulips from opening up, lay the stems flat on a hard surface, before arranging them, and with the point of a sharp knife, penetrate right through the stem of each flower in turn, about one inch below the flower head. It sounds brutal, and one does have to do it carefully, but the theory is that less water then arrives at the bud, causing it to remain closed. Since wide-open tulips in a vase don't appeal to me, I steel myself and pierce each tulip stem before I arrange them, and invariably it has worked for me. I also submerge the heads of hydrangeas completely under cold water for a few hours before arranging them. This hydrates them, and since hydrangeas love water (it is part of their name), they appreciate the submersion.

All flowers cut from shrubs (such as forsythia and flowering almond) and others with woody stems benefit from having the ends of their stems hammered or crushed. This allows the water to penetrate the outer covering of the stem so that more moisture is taken up. All flowers with stems that exude a milky substance (for example, euphorbia, poppy, and poinsettia) should, after picking, have the stem steeped in two inches of boiling water for a few seconds before they are conditioned in a container of deep, cool water. This seals the stems so that they don't leak sap, but the stems above the sealed ends will still take up water. Once an arrangement has been completed, never place it in a draft, near a radiator or fireplace where it gets direct heat, or near a window in direct sun.

ADAPTATIONS FROM JAPANESE DESIGNS

Choose containers that either blend or contrast with the colors of your plant material and also consider the line of the proposed arrangement in relation to the shape of the vase. Arrangements should have three dimensions, height, width, and depth, and the container is an integral part of the whole. The line of an arrangement may be symmetrical (for instance, an arc) or asymmetrical. A line design is different from mass designs in that fewer flowers are needed, but each item therefore must be more perfect. A line design, by definition, is an arrangement of flowers, leaves, twigs, and so on in which special attention is focused on the shape of the outline. Americans have learned a great deal from Japanese flower arrangers about the importance of this type of design, and tend to adapt the Japanese principles of using three curved bare branches cut to symbolize Heaven (*Shin*), Man (*Soe*), and Earth (*Hikae*). Heaven is traditionally cut so its height measures the width of the container plus its depth. Man is cut to measure three-quarters of the length of Heaven; Earth is cut to measure three-quarters of the length of Man.

In the nineteenth century, the Japanese began to use the shallow, flat containers that we most frequently associate with Japanese arrangements today. A pin-holder is placed right of center in these containers. The three branches are inserted into the back of the pin-holder with stems close together as if they were growing out of the same trunk. The branches are angled outward and slightly forward to the left as one looks at the arrangement. In descending heights, Heaven is the highest branch, followed by Man and then Earth. Perhaps three flowers and/or some leaves are then placed low in the arrangement, echoing the curve of the topmost (Heaven) branch. See below.

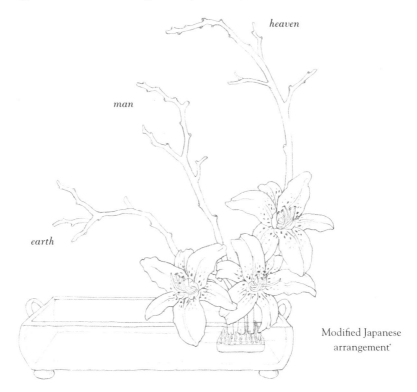

heaven

man

earth

Modified Japanese arrangement

An American line arrangement may only consist of one branch, with more flowers outlining the curve so that the end result is like a crescent moon or an L shape. So an asymmetrical arrangement built on a block of Oasis in a rectangular shallow bowl is often the easiest to manage. Place the tallest flower stem in the Oasis about three-quarters of the way along the container to the left. Then insert a medium-long stem into the side of the Oasis horizontally so that it extends out from the container on the right. Thus the height and the width of the arrangement are defined. Then place some of the largest blooms, with the stems cut short, at the base of the longest stem at the left to become the massed focal point. Place smaller flowers and greenery to define the L shape upwards and outwards. Odd numbers of flowers or leaves look best. The heaviest flower, in terms of both form and color, should be right on the rim of the container in the left corner of the L. All the flowers must face the front and at least one of the lower ones should be angled forward, almost at a right angle to the rim, to give a three-dimensional effect. See below.

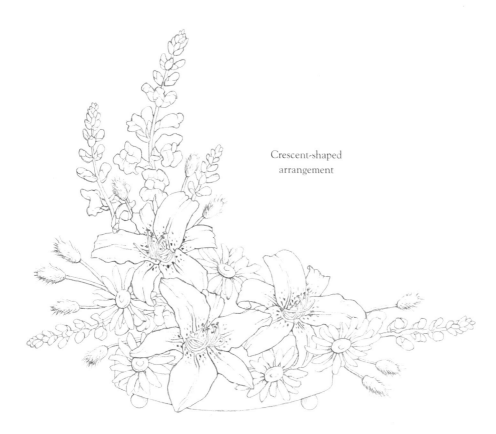

Crescent-shaped
arrangement

THE APPEAL OF COLOR

While line and design are the most important aspects of flower arranging in Japan, in the West, color is the most important. Color can be approached in a variety of ways: by considering the colors in the room in which the arrangement will be placed, by creating harmony through the choice of two colors near to one another in the color spectrum (such as violet and blue), or by using a variety of tones of one color, contrasting two or more colors, or using monochromatic materials or one's own favorite colors. It is all a matter of personal choice.

However, the distribution of color in an arrangement is very important, particularly in mass displays. The vitality of the arrangement depends on this distribution of color. Dark, rich colors attract the eye more rapidly than do light, delicate ones. So the visual center of groupings of colors should be in the middle and close to the base of the arrangement. Big, dark blooms have the most visual weight, so these need to be low and front and center, while small, feathery blooms or bare branches should be higher. Stems should be placed so that they appear to radiate from a central point in an arrangement, and stems should never cross each other. Rhythmic, graceful curves are most pleasing to the eye. However, it is the colors, and the way that they create either a gentle harmony or a dramatic contrast, that boost the visual appeal.

In our gardens most of us will have some hosta plants, and their leaves provide wonderful contrast for many perennial flowers. When we are choosing perennials to plant, we should always consider what their foliage will contribute both in the garden and in the vase.

CONTAINERS

Garage sales, thrift shops, and antique stores are all good sources of containers. I collect tiny perfume bottles for my miniature flower arrangements of the tiny spring bulbs. An arrangement of little flowers can tug at the heart, especially if the color of the container picks up or harmonizes with the flowers. Small arrangements can be grouped together or used singly. Lilies of the valley look pristine in a green, medium-sized glass container with a narrow neck. A few of their own green leaves at the sides of the grouping of flowers sets off their delicate nodding bells. Lenten roses (hellebores) last well floating in shallow bowls where one can look down on their unusual colors and markings. All members of the narcissus family combine well, and the blue of grape hyacinths is a good contrast with their yellows and whites. Branches of forsythia can be forced in a tall vase early in the spring when they are in bud. Just hammer the stems and place them in warm water inside, and the heat in the house will tease them into thinking that it is time to bloom. It may take up to three or four weeks, and the process is helped by changing the water in the vase frequently.

I have a medium-sized glass bowl, and it holds up to three stemless daylilies, though sometimes I put just one choice bloom into it. Each summer morning as I walk in my garden I select my "daylily of the day." I place it where I can look down into the lily's throat, and all day I admire it. In this way I feel I can experience, up close and personal, one example from each of the many varieties as they come into bloom. I used to use water in the bowl until I realized that their day of bloom is the same length with or without water. Although I love to have vases crammed with flowers all over my house, singleton flowers are a special pleasure, too. A single flower stands on its own merits and allows one to concentrate on it and savor its special characteristics. John Ruskin wrote: "We cannot fathom the mystery of a single flower, nor is it intended that we should. . . ."

Friends of mine who are not gardeners look at me strangely when I say I cannot bear to be away in September because that is when my fall asters bloom. However, if you are reading this book you probably understand. In fact, you may have said or will at some time say something similar. Once we have perennials in our gardens, we wait for each predictable flush of bloom like a lovesick teenager waiting for the phone to ring. The only month of the growing season when I can bear to leave my garden is July, because the Japanese beetles are there then and it can also be so hot that I stay inside. However, I still make dashes into the garden to get those gloriously brassy gold black-eyed Susans and some dark basil 'Opal' leaves, which I like to put with them. The arranging of cherished flowers is still a joy even in the humid hot weather. It is a special joy to arrange flowers from one's own garden. Flowers, after all, help us celebrate our joys and heal our sorrows. Anne Morrow Lindbergh, who certainly was acquainted with sorrow, summed up so eloquently, yet simply, what she felt when she wrote: "Arranging a bowl of flowers in the morning can give a sense of quiet in a crowded day—like writing a poem or saying a prayer."

DRYING AND PRESERVING FLOWERS

Many perennial flowers dry well and hold their color when they do. A perennial garden also provides material that can be harvested for potpourri. In fact it is easy to collect flower heads for potpourri in a basket when you are deadheading and leave them to dry for later. If flower heads are spread in the bottom of a large basket so that the air can circulate through the basket weave, they will dry and retain their color if kept in a dry, dark place.

Hanging Flowers to Dry

Hanging flowers to dry is an inexpensive and easy method of ensuring that you will have flowers from your garden to arrange for winter bouquets. In January, once the holiday decorations have been put away, it is especially satisfying to have dried flowers available to arrange. So during the summer and fall, pick some of the flowers in your garden and hang them to dry. Strip the leaves from each stem as you pick the flowers. This is necessary because the leaves get very brittle when they dry and can make the job of arranging dried bouquets quite messy. I just walk around my garden with some rubber bands on my wrist so that I can quickly bunch together the flowers I cut. It simplifies the process if you have some nails or hooks in a wall somewhere so that the flowers can easily be hung once they have been harvested. I hang my bunches of summer flowers on the hooks in front of my fireplace where the Christmas stockings are hung at Christmas. Once the bunches of flowers are dry, I remove them and stand them upright in vases in a dark closet. The reason bunches of flowers dry best upside down is that the stems dry straight, and this makes the flowers easier to arrange later. However, flowers with very stiff woody stems, such as hydrangeas, will dry well upright in a vase. Annuals such as blue salvia, statice, and purple and pink globe amaranth can be dried upside down combined in the same bunch, and this combination looks especially pretty. Celosia dries well, too, and often looks striking on its own in a vase.

Perennial flowers that dry well include alium, baby's breath, peony, yarrow (yellow), polyantha roses, globe thistle, goldenrod, ironweed, astilbe, lady's mantle, sea lavender, lavender, and lamb's ears. Artemesia provides good contrastive foliage. Seed heads from iris, clematis, columbine, grape hyacinth, honesty, poppy, and coneflower, as well as rose hips, can also be dried to add interesting additional accents to dried arrangements.

Always harvest materials to be dried in the morning: wait until the dew has evaporated, but pick the items before the sun gets too hot. Good air circulation is essential for plant material to dry well, and direct sun fades the colors. So inside the house, where it is air-conditioned, is preferable to a garage or shed where high humidity can retard the drying process and occasionally even cause mildew.

Dish Arrangements

Tiny rose buds, and even larger roses that have drooped in a vase but not opened fully before drooping, may be snipped off, so that little of the stem remains, and set upright in a small dish that has low sides to support a closely packed mass of heads. This dish-type arrangement of roses sitting upright will dry and retain color for months. When you tire of it, the dried roses can be added to potpourri.

Flowers from our own gardens, that we have dried ourselves, have special meaning for us. They have that slightly faded antique look that is often softer and more charming than the stronger colors seen in the dried flowers that are available in stores. Pressing flowers, such as pansies, and autumn leaves in an old phone book is also fun and easily accomplished. Leaves, such as those from beech trees (maples don't do as well) picked late in August or early September, but also other kinds of foliage, can be preserved, too. Split or crush the woody stems and place them in a jar containing one part glycerine to two parts water. The liquid should be about four inches deep. Put them in a place with good air circulation for two or three weeks. Once the glycerine has been absorbed, the foliage will last indefinitely. Remember that the fewer the stems, the narrower the neck of the container must be for them to be supported well and look pleasing in a vase.

In the following chapters you will find profiles of some special perennials that are recommended for the home gardener who loves to have cut flowers. These bloom reliably in regions with cold winters and are easygoing in terms of basic requirements.

Daffodil
Narcissus sp.

FIVE

Spring

WINTER ACONITE
Eranthis hyemalis

Eranthis

Pronounced: er-AN-this
Also known as: winter aconite
Family: *Renunculaceae*
Colors: yellow, white
Zones: 3–7

Description: There are about seven species of these low-growing perennials native to Europe and Asia. The leaves are palmate and dissected and look like a frill of green beneath the flowers, which are made up of five to eight sepals. The actual petals are modified into small nectaries. Though the small tubers are sold in bulb catalogs, aconites are best propagated by division.

Cultivation: *E. hiemalis* (hi-MAL-is) has sessile 2- to 6-inch-high yellow flowers in early spring, when it blooms with the snowdrops. It can be grown in zones 3–7 but likes cold and thrives in shaded moist sites. Since it is an ephemeral, it should be planted where it won't be disturbed when it dies down later in the season. It increases over time into colonies, and its acid-yellow blooms light up the landscape even amid patches of late snow during early spring thaws. Put a few little blooms in tiny bottles indoors so that you can admire them up close.

Eranthis is the Greek word for "spring flower." These are miniature flowers that singly or *en masse* perform each year for only a short time. When gardeners plant aconites, they can accumulate gold that is priceless. Susan Hill wrote, "of all human activities, apart from the procreation of children, gardening is the most optimistic and hopeful. The gardener is by definition one who plans for and believes and trusts in a future, whether in the short or longer term."

HELLEBORE
Helleborus orientalis

Helleborus

Pronounced:	hell-eh-BORE-us
Also known as:	Lenten rose, Christmas rose
Family:	*Renunculaceae*
Colors:	subtle variations of cream, chartreuse, dusty mauve, purple, creamy pink, and green
Zones:	4–9

Description: Perennials with robust rootstocks, native to limestone regions of Europe and Asia. The leaves are coarse and palmate and semi-evergreen. The flowers have five sepals and at their center are many stamens. The plants are poisonous, so deer avoid them.

Cultivation: *H. orientalis* (Lenten rose) grows best in full to light shade with rich and evenly moist, though well-drained, soil. Clumps spread about 1–1½ feet and like to be undisturbed. Dig self-sown seedlings in spring and summer to replant elsewhere. Move or divide mature plants only after they have bloomed but never divide *H. argutifolius* or *H. foetidus* (stinking hellebore), as the rhizomes of these species are too short to withstand division and grow only in zones 6–9. The dark green leathery leaves and the flowers that persist on the plants for a long time make all of the species and cultivars valuable in light to full shade. Cut off tattered, winter-damaged foliage in early spring.

The genus name *Helleborus* is from the Greek words *helein,* "to kill," and *bora,* meaning "food." The *H. niger* (Christmas rose) has black roots, and *H. foetidus* is so named because the leaves have an unpleasant scent when crushed. The blooms display well floating in a bowl so that the variations in their markings can be admired. The early timing of their appearance makes them treasured. An anonymous poet wrote,

> . . . this winter rose
> Blossoms amid the snows
> A symbol of God's promise, care and love.

RETICULATED IRIS
Iris reticulata

Iris reticulata

Pronounced:	EYE-riss
Also known as:	dwarf iris, miniature iris
Family:	*Iridaceae*
Colors:	blue, lilac, purple, white, yellow
Zones:	5–9

Description: There are about two hundred or more species of iris native to the North Temperate Zone. The genus is separated into two divisions: species with a rhizome (subgenus *Iris*), and species with a bulb (subgenera *Xiphium* and *Scorpiris*). *Xiphium* includes the English, Dutch, and Spanish irises, which have large erect standards (petals that point up and out) and smooth bulbs that have no roots when they are in the resting phase. The reticulated irises have a fibrous cover, like a network, on the bulbs. The stems are very short (3–6"), and these miniature irises bloom very early in the spring and are good companions for crocus. Dwarf iris have intricate patterns on their petals, and the bulbs are planted in the fall, preferably in drifts. The name is from the Latin word meaning "like a net."

Cultivation: Plant the *I. reticulata* bulbs 3 inches deep and 1 inch apart in a well-drained, sunny location. They dislike wet summers and must be dry during dormancy. After they bloom, leave the grassy foliage to die down naturally, so food is stored in the bulb for the following year, and apply some granular fertilizer after flowering. Flowers can be picked and displayed in tiny glass bottles so their intricate markings can be enjoyed indoors. These early bloomers are especially welcome as dainty harbingers of spring, and their luscious colors are a treat for winter-weary eyes. *Iris* is the sacred flower of the goddess of the rainbow, and it means "eye of heaven." It is also the name of the center of our eyes.

> Of course you'll laugh
> To think such a short iris
> Is reticulated like a
> TALL GIRAFFE!

CREEPING PHLOX
Phlox subulata

GH
2007

Phlox subulata

Pronounced: FLOCKS
Also known as: moss phlox, creeping phlox, moss pink
Family: *Polemoniaceae*
Colors: lavender, pink, purple, white, bi-color
Zones: 2–9

Description: Ground-hugging 2- to 6-inch-tall species forming 1½–2-foot mats with evergreen needle-like leaves and producing masses of small flowers in the spring. Native to North America, from New York to Maryland and west to Michigan.

Cultivation: *P. subulata* needs plenty of sun and reliable moisture and provides excellent ground cover that drapes over walls. The lavender seems to spread better than the other colors. These short plants provide a lovely mat of color in the spring. The name, *phlox*, is from a Greek word meaning "flame," as many of the original taller phlox were red. *Subulata* means "awl-shaped," and an awl is a small pointed tool, so the name probably refers to the needle-like leaves. White and paler phlox look luminous in the evening light. Plant *en masse* in various colors for the most dramatic effects. They combine well with *Iberis* and *Saponaria* on slopes and in rock gardens. Divide immediately after flowering or in the fall.

> Here I come creeping, creeping everywhere;
> My humble song of praise
> Most joyfully I raise
> To Him at whose command
> I beautify the land,
> Creeping, silently creeping everywhere.
>
> —*Sarah Roberts Boyle*

GRAPE HYACINTH
Muscari armeniacum

Muscari

Pronounced: muss-KAR-ee
Also known as: grape hyacinth, starch hyacinth
Family: *Liliaceace*
Colors: blue, white, bi-color
Zones: 2–8

Description: There are approximately forty species of these spring-flowering perennial bulbs, native to the Mediterranean regions and southwest Asia, that are useful for colonizing. The flower racemes, 6–8 inches tall, are composed of tight, almost-closed blossoms. They have long, narrow leaves. The small bulbs are planted in the fall.

Cultivation: For best effect, plant quantities of the bulbs M. *botryoides* 3 inches deep and 3 inches apart either in full sun or in partial shade, and allow the leaves to die back naturally after the flowers fade. Some people believe these flowers smell like starch. They naturalize well under trees and shrubs and can also be used as edging for beds. Some have foliage that appears in the fall, so M. *armeniacum,* for example, can be used as a marker if it is planted with other spring-blooming bulbs that have foliage that emerges only in the spring. This enables the gardener to avoid digging at a later time in a place where bulbs are already in the ground.

Muscari is from the Greek *moschos,* meaning "musk," and most grape hyacinth have a sweet, musky scent which is not attractive to deer. The species name *botryoides* is Greek for "a bunch of grapes." The name comes from the flower spires' texture and from the way the erect spike resembles that of other types of hyacinth. Grape hyacinth combine well in beds and in a vase with all other spring-blooming bulbs, as they provide a heavenly touch of blue. Blue flowers like these bring bits of heaven down into our gardens.

VIRGINIA BLUEBELLS
Mertensia virginica

Mertensia

Pronounced:	mer-TEN-see-uh
Also known as:	Virginia bluebell, Virginia cowslip, lungwort, Roanoke bells
Family:	*Boraginaceae*
Colors:	blue, pink, white, lilac-blue
Zones:	3–8

Description: M. *virginica* (vir-GIN-ic-uh) is native to North America, from New York state south to Tennessee and west to Kansas. The genus name honors an early German botanist, Franz Karl Mertens. The smooth, ovate, blue-green leaves alternate along the fleshy fragile stem. Loose clusters of tubular pink buds open into porcelain blue nodding flowers, each on its own stalk. The flare of the bell has five pleats. The first detailed description of this plant was made from a specimen collected in Virginia. This plant has more recently been classified as M. *pulmonarioides* (pul-moe-nair-ee-OY-deez), and the common name lungwort refers to its resemblance to a European species that was once thought to cure lung disorders. It is best propagated by seed, so do not cut off the seed heads. It naturalizes well in woodland sites. If transplanted, which is problematic, it must be dug deeply so that a clump of earth is attached.

Cultivation: Select a site in filtered sun or light shade with rich, evenly moist, well-drained soil in a spot where its gnarled tuberous roots will not be inadvertently disturbed when this plant disappears after its spring display. Combine with pulmonaria, ferns, or other shade lovers to cover their absence later in the season.

> A Blue Bell nodding down
> Demure in her Alice-blue gown

CELANDINE POPPY
Stylophorum diphyllum

Chelidonium

Pronounced:	Kel-ih-DOH-nee-um
Also known as:	celandine poppy, killwort, swallowwort, wartwort, wood poppy
Family:	*Pavaveraceae*
Color:	yellow
Zones:	5–8

Description: A wildflower native to Europe and western Asia that has naturalized throughout North America. Pinnate leaves are divided into lobes, and broken stems exude an orange sap. Flowers have four yellow petals and two green sepals and appear from the axils of the upper leaves in loose clusters. The seeds are contained in fuzzy capsules. *C. majus* (MAY-jus) may have been brought to America by pioneer doctors, as the juice was used for warts and corns. A native celandine poppy is *Stylophorum diphyllum*, and it is difficult to distinguish between *Chelidonium* and *Stylophorum*. However, neither is as invasive as is a plant, native to Europe, known as the lesser celandine.

Cultivation: The celandine poppy will grow almost anywhere but it is happiest in partial shade, where it enthusiastically self-sows, which is fortunate since the plants tend to be short-lived. Their cheerful flowers and decorative foliage make them invaluable in shade gardens. They grow from a fleshy perennial rootstock into 1½–2-foot-tall yellowy green clumps, and so combine well with pulmonaria, ferns, dicentra, brunnera, astilbe, and hosta. 'Flora Pleno' bears double flowers, and while the main flush is in the spring, celandine poppies continue to throw blooms throughout the season. *Chelidonium* is from the Greek *chelidon,* meaning "swallow," because the plants flower from the time swallows arrive in the spring to when they depart in the fall. These easy-care plants are untroubled by pests, and extra plants can be easily dug to pass along to other gardeners. Their fuzzy seed pods are an extra bonus and a feature to show to children. There is a happy exuberance in a shade garden that provides a home for these uncomplicated poppies.

CANDYTUFT
Iberis sempervirens

Iberis

Pronounced: eye-BEER-ISS
Also known as: candytuft, candyedge
Family: *Brassicaceae*
Color: white
Zones: 3–9

Description: There are many annual, perennial, and sub-shrub members of the genus and the ones we grow are perennial sub-shrubs with rounded clusters of small flowers and linear to ovate leaves. They like alkaline, well-drained soils and are native to central Europe, the Mediterranean, and North Africa. The perennial forms are white bloomers, and the annual plants are often pink or purple.

Cultivation: Plant in full sun or very light shade. Wet soil in winter causes them to rot, so they do well in a raised bed or on a slope. After they have flowered in the spring, cut plants back one-third to remove spent flowers as they quickly go to seed. Every few years cut them back by two-thirds to keep plants compact. They may be rooted from cuttings in the spring or early summer. *I. saxatilis* (sax-ah-TILL-iss) is a low-growing sub-shrub which spreads about 1 foot, with evergreen needle leaves, in zones 2–7. *I. sempervirens* (sem-per-VYE-rens) is also an evergreen sub-shrub about 1 foot high and 1½ feet wide. 'Little Gem' is a dwarf (6" tall) and 'Autumn Beauty' and 'Autumn Snow' are both re-bloomers in zones 3–9. All are effective in rock gardens or for draping over walls, and the compact forms make excellent edging plants.

The name *Iberis* is the ancient name for Spain, which is the source of several species. The English common name is a corruption of *Candia*, the ancient name for Crete: hence the "tufted plant from Candia" became candytuft. It was once used to treat rheumatism and therefore was often represented in herb gardens in olden times. The frothy white flower heads are a good foil for tulips in the spring garden, and the green foliage is an attractive ground cover once bloom is past. Short plants with masses of white flowers provide a lacy romantic touch in a garden.

Sounds like Candy
Looks like lace
Adds romance
Anyplace.

CATMINT
Nepeta x faassenii

Nepeta

Pronounced: NEP-uh-tuh
Also known as: catmint
Family: *Lamiaceae*
Colors: lavender, purple, white
Zones: 4–8

Description: There are approximately 250 species of these aromatic, mostly perennial herbs, native to dry regions of Europe, Asia, and Africa. Stems are usually square with opposing greyish leaves and tubular flowers with two lips. Since they are members of the mint tribe they are vigorous, but thankfully deer are not attracted to them.

Cultivation: Nepetas are easily grown from seed or division. They grow in full sun or light shade in average well-drained soil. They will rot in damp conditions. Shear plants back hard after the spring bloom to encourage fresh foliage and flowers throughout the growing season. They are easily dug up if they need to be restrained, though they make a wonderful ground cover and edging that stifles weeds and shrugs off heat and drought. *N. cataria* (cah-TAR-ee-uh) is not especially ornamental and grows to 3 feet, but cats love it. *N. × faassenii* (fahs-SEN-ee-eye) is shorter, with long-blooming lavender-blue flowers, and 'White Wonder' and 'Snowflake' are good whites. While nepetas are considered homely by some, they provide the grey foliage advocated by Gertrude Jekyll, are useful underplantings for roses, clematis, and mallows, and have a softening effect in a border. They have been used for centuries in herb gardens and for medicinal purposes. The foliage is useful as filler in small flower arrangements. Easy-care plants such as nepeta pay their way in a garden.

Of lineage
Undistinguished . . .
But maintenance free
You'll agree!

Foxglove

Digitalis grandiflora

SIX

Summer

CRANESBILL GERANIUM
Geranium 'Rozanne'

Geranium

Pronounced:	jer-AY-nee-um
Also known as:	cranesbill, true geranium, hardy or wild geranium
Family:	*Geraniaceae*
Colors:	magenta, pink, purple, violet-blue, white
Zones:	4–8
Height:	up to 2 feet

Description: These are mostly short-statured, long-lived perennials with mounds of palmate (hand-like) leaves that are often toothed or lobed. Some species have colorful fall foliage. Blooms are simple cups with five petals. Members of the species may be tender or hardy and some may be evergreen in mild areas. Native to Europe, they are sometimes confused with the annual pelargoniums from South Africa which are also referred to as geraniums and are grown in pots during the summer. All are easy-care and pest-free.

Cultivation: They thrive in full sun or partial shade, though in hot summers they enjoy more protection from the sun. After the first flush of bloom (usually spring) is past, cut them back to an inch from the ground, and new leaves will grow and some varieties will re-bloom. Divide them in spring or fall. Useful as ground cover to discourage weeds, they combine well with dicentra, pulmonaria, celandine poppy, and coral bells in light shade. They are staples in cottage gardens and are pass-along plants.

The name comes from the Greek word meaning "crane," as their seed pods are pointed like a crane's bill.

There are so many different cranesbill geraniums, and some newer varieties such as *G. rozeanne* bloom repeatedly all summer. If many different varieties are planted, these serviceable yet dainty flowering plants can supply lots of blooms in a garden. Since they come in pinks, blues, and purples, they are good interwoven around the skirts of taller perennials in a soft-hued perennial bed, and their foliage is attractive, too. They combine especially well with pink and white roses if a romantic look is desired—for example, at the base of an arch or trellis.

> The humble cranesbill
> Creeps and weaves
> Covers the ground
> And stifles weeds.

GAS PLANT
Dictamnus albus

Dictamnus

Pronounced:	dick-TAM-nus
Also known as:	gasplant, dittany, fraxinella, candle plant
Family:	*Rutaceae* (contains only one species)
Colors:	pink, white (*D. albus*), and purplish pink (*D. albus* 'Purpureus') with darker veins
Zones:	3–8
Height:	1½–3 feet

Description: A long-lived tall perennial herb with strong stems and glossy pinnately compound leaves. Pinnate leaves are leaves on either side of a stem in a feather-like arrangement. It bears terminal racemes of small fragrant flowers in early summer. Native to areas from southern Europe through northern China.

Cultivation: Grows in full sun or light shade in rich, well-drained soil and will rot in poorly drained areas. Plants establish slowly, take three to four years to begin blooming well, and are difficult to transplant successfully. *Dictamnus* is drought-tolerant once established. Propagates by seed.

These plants exude a volatile oil which, when the weather is humid, may ignite if a lighted match is held nearby. This foliage oil may also cause a rash, if gloves are not worn or if the gardener is susceptible.

Dictamnus rewards the gardener who sites it with care and is patient enough to wait for it to become established. It makes a strong statement when it blooms as it forms a 3-foot-wide clump that is both long-enduring and statuesque, drawing all eyes to its multiple flower spires, which persist for some weeks. Give it space so that it becomes a focal point and a conversation piece for garden visitors. It is not a well-known plant and it is not possible to divide an established plant, though it is available through mail order catalogs. It is best to leave the flower spikes on the plant, as they persist for a very long time in the garden, where the vertical spikes provide an architectural effect and the seed pods can be used in dried arrangements.

> Gas plant is an unfortunate name.
> I wonder who should get the blame?
> Yet, no matter who's to blame
> It will be called that, just the same.

BEE BALM
Monarda didyma
'CAMBRIDGE SCARLET'

GH
2007

Monarda

Pronounced:	mo-NAR-duh
Also known as:	bergamot, bee balm, horsemint
Family:	*Labiatae*
Colors:	shades of pink, red, and magenta, purple, violet, and white
Zones:	4–8
Height:	2 feet

Description: Perennial aromatic herbs native across North America and Mexico. The stems are mostly square with pungent opposing leaves and shaggy flowers, often with a ring of bracts, and attractive to butterflies and bees. They spread readily, as they belong to the mint clan, which means that they are vigorous but not attractive to deer. They are used for flavoring teas and are beloved by bees.

Cultivation: All members of the genus grow rapidly in sun or light shade and are more aggressive in moist soil. They are susceptible to powdery mildew. Propagate by division, as they need dividing frequently to keep them vigorous and within bounds, or let them naturalize on the edge of a woods. They are the quintessential pass-along plant, as anyone who grows them eventually has too much. If you have an out-of-the-way spot where monarda can romp on its own you won't have to divide it so often.

Cultivars include M. *didyma* (DID-i-ma), M. 'Cambridge Scarlet', and the mildew-resistant 'Jacob Cline', 'Marshall's Delight', 'Prairie Night', and 'Petite Delight'. The bright, shaggy flowers can be cut for bouquets. They are a magnet for hummingbirds.

> Hummingbirds dart,
> Seduced by Monarda's
> Sweet vivid heart.

SHASTA DAISY
Leucanthemum superbum
'BECKY'

Shasta Daisy

Pronounced:	SHASS-tuh
Also known as:	chrysanthemum, Nippon daisy
Family:	*Compositae*
Color:	white
Zones:	4–8
Height:	1–4 feet

Description: Perennial daisies native mostly to the Northern Hemisphere. They are hardy, strong, aromatic plants with yellow disc flowers in the center of the blooms, surrounded by white ray flowers. There are many cultivars, and most produce single daisy flowers, but some are double. The genus *Leucanthemum* (leu-CAN-thuh-mum) is made up of twenty-six species of white daisies which used to be subsumed under the genus *Chrysanthemum*. What we call Shasta daisies are hybrids developed by crosses of *Leucanthemum maximum* with *L. lacustre*. They first naturalized on the slopes of Mount Shasta in Washington state. There are many Shasta daisy cultivars, with plants ranging from 1 to 4 feet. The leaves are dark green and may be lobed, toothed, or scalloped. The flowers are borne at the tips of the stems and are usually solitary.

Cultivation: These plants need a site in full sun and rich, well-drained soil (especially in winter). Pinch back to encourage compact growth, deadhead, and divide clumps every two to three years in the spring. 'Little Miss Muffet' is a low-grower, and 'Becky' has stiff substance and so does not need staking. These daisies are long-lived cut flowers that combine well with other blooms in a vase. The clean-looking foliage of Shasta daisies is a bonus in the garden during hot weather, and of course the flowers look crisp and cool also. These are refined-looking flowers that are larger and have stronger stems than wild daisies.

Surely, every gardener hasta
Plant at least one white Shasta!

MOONBEAM COREOPSIS
Coreopsis verticillata 'Moonbeam'

Coreopsis

Pronounced:	cor-ee-OP-sis
Also known as:	tickseed
Family:	*Compositae*
Colors:	primarily yellow, orange, rose, brown, or bi-color
Zones:	4–9
Height:	1–2½ feet

Description: There are more than one hundred species of annuals and perennials native to North and South America and Africa. Leaves may be lance-like or thread-like, opposite or alternate on upright stems. Flowers are disc-like, similar to daisies in form, and all varieties grow easily from seed and are long-blooming.

Cultivation: Plants are pest-free and love sun and heat, though C. *auriculata* and C. *rosea* will grow in partial shade. Once established, coreopsis will withstand drought, and soil should not be too rich. Deadhead to prolong bloom and shear off the thread-leaf varieties (C. *verticillata*), which spread via rhizomes to form 3-foot clumps. 'Moonbeam' is a pale yellow, 1-foot variety that does not need deadheading as it flowers all summer. 'Zagreb' is a vigorous thread-leaf variety with golden flowers on 1½-foot plants and is a good selection for wildflower plantings rather than a border. C. *lanceolata* has broader leaves and has been hybridized to provide both single and double and bi-color flowers. Easily grown, varieties may be dwarf or up to 2½ feet tall. Divide every two to three years in spring or fall to maintain vigor.

Coreopsis plants are known for their sunny disposition and yield good cut flowers to pop into a simple glass jar for a natural, cheerful-looking bouquet.

The genus name is from the Latin word for "bug" because the seeds are black and hooked, and look like insects. Fortunately it is a plant that is generally not referred to by its common name, as "coreopsis" definitely sounds more appealing than "tickseed."

There is smiling summer here . . .

—*Emily Dickinson*

ASTILBE
Astilbe x arendsii 'FANAL'

Astilbe

Pronounced:	uh-STILL-bee
Also known as:	goat's beard
Family:	*Saxifragaceae*
Colors:	white, pink, rose, maroon, purple
Zones:	3–8
Height:	1–6 feet

Description: Astilbes are moisture-loving perennials with rhizome-type roots that form 1–3-foot clumps. They have ferny foliage and feathery panicles of tiny flowers. They are native to North America and Eastern Asia. They have been heavily hybridized so that there are many early-, mid-, and late-season-blooming cultivars derived from Astilbe × *arendsii* or A. *japonica*.

Cultivation: They flourish in rich, moist, well-drained soil that is partially shaded. With adequate moisture they will grow in full sun, but in hot summers prefer afternoon shade. Browning of leaf edges indicates either insufficient moisture or inadequate shade. Mulch well, as this helps conserve moisture. Divide every few years in spring or early fall. Many cultivars are available and planting a number of different cultivars can ensure bloom across the growing season. For example, A. 'Deutschland' is a white early bloomer, A. 'Bridal Veil' blooms mid-season, and the scarlet A. 'Red Sentinel' blooms late. Chinese astilbe, A. *chinensis var. pumila* (chi-NEN-SIS), is a dwarf and a vigorous spreader with compact pink-purple panicles of flowers in late summer. A. *chinensis* 'Davidii' grows 4–6 feet, with handsome bronze foliage and purplish-pink flower panicles.

Astilbes combine well with lady's mantle, maidenhair fern, wild geranium, hosta, annual impatiens, and hellebores, and will flourish in dappled shade under deciduous trees as long as they get sufficient moisture. Few shade-loving perennials provide such a variety of both colors and bloom times. The flower spires also provide a good contrast with the flowers of low-growing shade lovers. Astilbes blooming amid low-growing woodland plants look like church steeples among a village of round green houses, as their spires grow up above their neighbors. One color planted *en masse* is especially effective.

> The plants suck in the earth, and are
> With constant drinking fresh and fair
>
> —*Abraham Cowley*

PURPLE CONEFLOWER
Echinacea purpurea

Echinacea

Pronounced:	eck-in-AY-see-uh, also eck-i-NAY-shuh
Also known as:	coneflower, red sunbonnet, droops, Indian root
Family:	*Compositae*
Colors:	purple, pink, white, orange
Zones:	3–9
Height:	1–4 feet

Description: These are North American natives with stiff, coarse stems and leaves and daisy-type flowers with petals that droop down from raised, spiny, cone-shaped centers made up of orangey disk florets.

Cultivation: All tried and true varieties, *E. angustifolia* (rose pink), *E. pallida* (pale pink), and *E. purpurea* (purple), enjoy full sun and average soil. They are tolerant of heat and drought and may be divided in spring or fall. Heights range from 1 to 4 feet depending on the cultivar. Deadhead to maintain continuity of bloom through the summer. The flowers and seed heads attract birds and butterflies. Some cultivars are more compact, and 'White Swan', for example, grows 1–2 feet. Recent new cultivars include 'Pink Double Delight', 'Summer Sky', and 'Harvest Moon', extending the range of colors and forms.

The name is from the Greek *echinos*, meaning "hedgehog," because of the spiny texture of the flower's center. Coneflowers frequently self-sow, and new plants are best transplanted when they are small and their taproots are easier to dislodge. Plants will bloom in light shade but will get leggy, and so need to be pinched back. Coneflowers provide welcome color in the hottest part of the summer. Like all daisy-type flowers they are useful as cut flowers in informal bouquets. The plant has been used medicinally for colds, snakebites, and scurvy. It is also one of the very easiest perennials to grow in the Midwest.

Stalwart, high-centered flowers
Unfazed by scarce summer showers.

HOSTA
Hosta 'Royal Standard'

Hosta

Pronounced:	HOSS-tuh
Also known as:	plantain lilies, August lilies, funkia
Family:	*Liliaceae*
Colors:	white, lavender, and purple shades
Zones:	3–8
Height:	1–4 feet

Description: There are about seventy species native to Japan, China, and Korea. The plants form large clumps of attractive foliage and produce flower racemes 24–36 inches tall, though there are shorter and even miniature varieties. Foliage colors range through dark green, blue-green, green-grey, and chartreuse, with interesting leaf shapes and color combinations. Flowers come in white and also a wide range of hues from palest lavender to deepest purple.

Cultivation: Select a site in light to full shade that has even moisture for best results. Blue-leaved cultivars generally show their best color with no direct sun, while golden-leaved cultivars tolerate more sun. Bright, dappled shade is best for those with variegated leaves, though usually hostas are forgiving plants. Cut the bloom stems back after flowering and propagate by division. They look best *en masse* and can be used to good effect as edgings for shady beds or as single-species beds encircling deciduous trees. They make good ground covers, as they deter weeds. All are hardy in zones 3–8.

Originally funkia, the name was changed to hosta to honor Nicholas Host (1761–1834), who was an Austrian physician. The common name of plantain lily was arrived at because hosta leaves resemble those of the plantain. Hosta hybrids and clumps can be as wide as they are tall. The smallest miniatures are popular in tiny gardens.

Hybridizers have been producing exciting crosses of these versatile yet serviceable plants. The names that have been given to them provide fascinating examples of the linguistic creativity of horticulturalists. Examples include 'Hanky Panky', 'Blue Mouse Ears', 'Blue Umbrellas', 'Ivory Coast', 'Big Daddy', 'Guacamole', and 'Zounds'.

> They won't be affected
> If they are neglected
> But try to be fair
> Give them some care . . .

GLOBE THISTLE
Echinops bannaticus
'TAPLOW BLUE'

Echinops

Pronounced: EEK-in-ops
Also known as: globe thistle
Family: *Compositae*
Colors: blue, white, violet-blue
Zones: 3–9
Height: 1½–6 feet

Description: There are about one hundred species of biennial and perennial plants native to hot dry areas, such as gravel slopes and grasslands, from the western Mediterranean region to central Asia. The leaves are pinnate and dissected with prickly margins. The flowers of the cultivated varieties such as *E. bannaticus* (ban-NAT-ih-kus) 'Taplow Blue' are a metallic blue.

Cultivation: These plants need good drainage, especially in winter, and once established they are very drought-tolerant and very hardy. They can grow up to 6 feet high and make an architectural statement in the garden. *E. ritro* (REE-tro) is a compact 2 feet, with a spread of 1½ feet, and if deadheaded it will re-bloom well with dark blue flower globes. *Echinops* plants resent being transplanted and can be left undisturbed for years. They readily self-seed, but the cultivars don't come true. The name *Echinops* is from the Greek *echinos*, for "hedgehog," and *opsis*, for appearance. The flower heads do well in both fresh and dried arrangements as the stems are stiff and insert easily into Oasis, and the metallic blue combines well with other hues. The flower heads resemble a mace, which is a spiked armor-breaking club used in the Middle Ages.

> Oh why, we ask, reversing good intentions,
> Was Nature so ingenious in inventions. . . .
> —*Vita Sackville-West*

This plant is an attention-grabber in a garden, provides architectural interest, and never needs staking. It is pest-free, and easy-care.

BLACK-EYED SUSAN
Rudbeckia fulgida

Rudbeckia

Pronounced:	rude-BECK-ee-uh
Also known as:	black-eyed Susans, orange coneflowers, helianthus
Family:	*Compositae*
Colors:	yellow, red-brown, bi-colors
Zones:	3–9
Height:	2–6 feet

Description: There are about twenty-five species of these coarse-leaved annual, biennial, or perennial North American natives with yellow to red-brown flowers. Daisy-type flower heads have fertile disc flowers (black, brown, or green) at the center with ray flowers (petals) surrounding them. The disc florets produce the seeds and are also responsible for the most common black-eye, referred to in the popular name.

Cultivation: Perennial rudbeckias are hardy in zones 3–9 and grow in full sun or light shade, though they perform best in sun. They are the easiest of perennials to grow, and most multiply rapidly, as they self-sow. While they prefer moist soil, they tolerate drought once they are established. As with other robust perennials, it is sometimes suggested that they may be more contained if planted in less than ideal soil. It is good to let them romp, so place them where they won't overpower better-behaved companions. By a fence, by a garage on their own, they need virtually no care except to be cut down when the plants are spent. Yet in July, their gold splashes of bright color are breathtaking. They last best in a vase when the stems are cut so that each flower has its own stem (about 9"), as flowers wilt if they are on tall, branched stems. Black-eyed Susans make cheerful bouquets either alone or combined with other summer garden flowers. The simplest flowers speak the most directly to the heart. Summer is not summer, unless there are some yellow daisies in the garden.

COMMON MALLOW
Malva sylvestris 'ZEBRINA'

Malva

Pronounced:	MAL-vuh
Also known as:	musk mallow, tree mallow, cheeses (the seeds look like cheese wheels)
Family:	*Malvaceae*
Colors:	rose, pink, maroon, white, blue-purple
Zones:	4–8
Height:	2–4 feet

Description: There are about thirty species of annuals, biennials, and perennials native to Europe, North Africa, and temperate Asia, and they are closely related to *Hibiscus*. Leaves of these plants are mostly large, rounded, and dark green, and blooms are cup-shaped with five petals, borne singly at the leaf axils.

Cultivation: Grow in full sun to partial shade in average, well-drained soil. Plants tend to be short-lived, but they self-sow, and plants transplant best if they are very small. M. *alcea* (al-SEE-uh) is the hollyhock mallow, growing up to 4 feet and forming 2-foot clumps. The musk mallow (M. *moschate*, moe-SHA-tuh) is hardiest and is 3 feet tall with pink or white flowers. M. *Sylvestris* (sil-VES-tris), or cheese mallow, is 3–4 feet and in bloom from late spring to fall. Plant 'Alba' or 'Primley Blue' or the striped 'Zebrina', whose pink/maroon blooms contrast well with the rich green of the leaves. These beauties are easily grown and provide vibrant color (and more plants) throughout the growing season.

> As soon as I'd seen her
> I bought sweet Zabrina.
> I thought one was plenty
> But now I have twenty!
> She's a profligate tart
> Who has stolen my heart!

HARDY BEGONIA
Begonia grandis

Hardy Begonia

Pronounced:	bih-GOAN-yah
Also known as:	[no alternative names]
Family:	*Begoniaceae*
Colors:	pink, white
Zones:	5–10
Height:	1–2 feet

Description: There are more than one thousand species of *Begonia* found in tropical and sub-tropical areas of both hemispheres. Most of these fleshy plants are grown in temperate zones as annuals or house plants. *B. grandis* ssp. *evansiana* (GRAN-diss ssp. ee-van-see-AH-nuh) grows outdoors in zones 5–10 and is an attractive addition to shade gardens. It grows from a tiny tuber, breaks dormancy late in the spring, and has handsome angel-wing-type leaves, often with red veins and undersides. In late summer it bears drooping clusters of pink flowers, though there is a variety, *alba*, which has white flowers. The plant develops small bulblets in its leaf axils which can grow into new plants.

Cultivation: The plants grow up to 2 feet, spread well if there is even moisture, and are partial to full shade, though in areas with cooler summers they will grow in sun. Female flowers have a winged seed capsule behind the petals which is absent in the male flowers, though both are usually seen on the same plant. Plants may be transplanted in summer or fall, and they also self-sow. Dig them with clumps of soil attached to the roots so that the tiny tubers aren't disturbed. They are available by mail from Wayside Gardens in North Carolina, and are advertised in their catalog, www.waysidegardens.com.

The entire family of begonias, those with fibrous roots, rhizomes, and tubers, are attractive plants named after Michel Bégon, who was a French civil servant and amateur botanist. Begonias were introduced in the United States in 1880 and immediately became popular, as they are both attractive and easy to propagate. A hardy begonia is unusual, but a wonderful addition to the garden, since it naturalizes well in woodland settings and grows up as early spring bulbs are dying down.

Despite its beauty and the fact that it begins blooming in late August, hardy begonia is not as widely grown by perennial gardeners as it deserves to be. The leaves as well as the flowers are charming. This is a plant no serious perennial gardener should be without.

> Dormant such a long while
> In Spring, yet after they appear
> Bloom into fall, and smile.

Blanket flower

Gaillardia aristata

SEVEN

Autumn

JAPANESE ANEMONE
Anemone tomentosa 'Robustissima'

Japanese Anemone

Pronounced:	ah-NEM-oh-nee
Also known as:	windflower, lily-of-the-field
Family:	*Ranunculaceae*
Colors:	pink, white, rose
Zones:	4–8
Height:	2½–5 feet

Description: There are approximately 120 species of perennial types of anemones, native mostly to the North Temperate Zone, often to mountainous regions. Leaves are usually more or less divided and form a ring below the flowers, which are held high in umbels on stiff stems. Their sepals are the showy part of the flower and there are no actual petals, but many stamens and pistils. The fall-blooming tall anemones are usually referred to as Japanese anemones (*A. japonica*) and are single pink flowers that were first found growing near Shanghai by Robert Fortune, a nineteenth-century plant explorer. The current name derives from the fact that they grow well in Japan. Some are hybrids and spread by rhizomes to form large clumps. 'Honorine Jobert' is white, 'Queen Charlotte' is a semi-double pink cultivar, and 'Margareta' is a double pink. *A. tomentosa var.* 'Robustissima' is the most hardy and adaptable.

Cultivation: These fall bloomers like full sun or partial shade and well-drained soil. In areas with hot summers they need afternoon shade and consistent moisture or the leaves will crisp. However, they are forgiving and exuberant plants that spread, and so are best planted in a bed of their own or divided often. They provide lots of color as other plants are winding down. The delicate flowers shatter easily, but after the petals fall the umbels with green centers can be used as greenery in flower arrangements. The single flowers of Japanese anemones are so simple and yet so elegant.

Do not confuse these with *Anemone blanda* (Grecian windflower), which are spring-flowering low-growing plants grown from bulbs. They are also useful additions to the perennial garden and have small, daisy-like flowers in blue, pink, or white, and ferny foliage. Use them to edge spring beds.

> And where a tear has dropped
> a windflower blows.
>
> —*Traditional saying*

SEDUM
Sedum 'VERA JAMESON'

Sedum

Pronounced:	SEE-dum
Also known as:	stonecrop, orpine
Family:	*Crassulaceae*
Colors:	pink, rose, red, yellow, white
Zones:	3–9
Height:	ground-hugging to 2½ feet

Description: There are approximately six hundred species of these succulents, which are native to the North Temperate Zone. There is great diversity in their habits, and the perennials most often grown in gardens range from mat-forming ground covers to 2½-foot-tall specimens suitable for beds and borders. There are clump-forming tall hybrids such as 'Autumn Joy' and 'Matrona', with showy flower heads composed of masses of tiny star-shaped flowers. S. 'Black Jack' has purplish black foliage which contrasts well with *Perovskia* (Russian sage) and fall-blooming asters. Since flower heads remain long into the fall, tall sedums make a significant contribution to the autumn garden display, often turning deeper in color as the air cools. They also attract butterflies.

Cultivation: Plant in full sun in well-drained soil. Low-growing sedums tolerate poor, dry soil and are good edgings for beds bordering concrete sidewalks. Some are invasive, so use these on their own. Cut the tall ones to the ground in early spring and propagate by division or cuttings. S. *spectabile* 'Brilliant' has hot pink flowers, and 'Variegata' has attractive cream and green leaves. S. *sieboldii* grows 6–9 inches tall and has pink flowers in the fall. Most are hardy to zones 3–9. The taller sedums need some support to remain erect but are splendid in the bed or border.

The name is from the Latin word *seob*, which means "to calm" or "to allay." The Romans grew sedum on their roofs to ward off lightning. While it doesn't provide this type of protection for perennial gardens, it may help with the water bill.

> You are not proud: you know your birth:
> For your embroider'd garments are from earth.
>
> —*Henry King*

PURPLE
FALL-BLOOMING ASTER
Aster novae-angliae

Fall-Blooming Aster

Pronounced:	ASS-ter
Also known as:	Michaelmas daisy, starwort (England and Germany), frost flower, eye of Christ
Family:	*Compositae*
Colors:	Purple, lavender, blue, pink, red, white
Zones:	3–8
Height:	1–5 feet

Description: There are about five hundred species of asters native to North and South America, Europe, Asia, and Africa. Named cultivars are grown from divisions, as seeds do not reproduce true to type. Like daisies, the small flowers consist of ray florets, which are the petals, surrounding the disc florets which make up the center. The blooms are mostly produced in clusters and the leaves are generally lance-shaped. They grow by creeping rhizomes and form large clumps. The name is the Latin word for "star." They combine well with sedums, joe-pye weed, and goldenrod.

Cultivation: Many cultivars have been developed from natives. Their American parents are known as our New England asters (A. *novae-angliae*) and New York asters (A. *novi-belgii*). Mulch the asters to help retain moisture. Cut them back to keep them more compact and divide regularly to maintain vigor. Low-growing 'Purple Dome' and 'Niobe' (white) do not need staking. Asters are easily grown and light up the fall garden with vibrant color. Give them plenty of space, for good air circulation prevents powdery mildew. Provide regular moisture to avoid browning of the lower leaves. In America they were considered roadside weeds until the English gardeners adopted them and new varieties were developed especially for gardens. They bloom at the time of the feast of St. Michael, thus the name "Michaelmas daisies," by which they are known in England.

> The scarlet of the maples
> can shake me like a cry of bugles going by.
> And my lonely spirit thrills
> To see the frosty asters like a smoke upon the hills
>
> —*Bliss Carman*

GARDEN
CHRYSANTHEMUM
Chrysanthemum morifolium

Chrysanthemum

Pronounced:	Kris-AN-the-mum
Also known as:	mums
Family:	*Compositae*
Colors:	all colors except blue
Zones:	4–9
Height:	1 foot

Description: There are between one hundred and two hundred species, mostly native to the Northern Hemisphere, where they are grown primarily as ornamentals. Pyrethrum is grown for insecticidal properties and one species is grown as a leaf vegetable in Asia. All have aromatic foliage and daisy, button, spider, spoon, pompom, quill, single, or double blooms. They were introduced to the United States in 1798, but they are very ancient plants—Confucius wrote about them in 500 BC. Their seeds went to Japan via Korea as early as the fourth century, and the Japanese revere the chrysanthemum as their imperial symbol. The Korean mums are of the daisy type, pink and apricot in color, and are the last flowers to bloom in Midwest gardens. 'Sheffield' and 'Single Apricot' are very hardy and their flowers last two weeks in a vase.

Cultivation: Chrysanthemums like full sun, and well-drained average to rich soil. Mums that are in flower when purchased and planted in the fall often don't have time to get their roots established, and so often don't winter over. Get divisions of hardy mums from friends or plant small plants of hardy varieties in the spring and pinch them back until July 4th to keep them compact. Mums are light-sensitive and start to set their buds as the days begin to shorten. Florist mums are not generally good candidates for our perennial gardens. Extend the fall bloom by planting early-, mid-, and late-fall bloomers that are hardy in your area.

When Autumn skies are clear and blue
When the air is crisp and bright
'Sheffield daisies' spring-like hue
Paints the earth with pink delight.

'SHEFFIELD PINK'

Appendix A
Plants That Prefer Constant Moisture

BOTANICAL NAME	COMMON NAME
Aruncus	goat's beard
Astilbe	hybrids
Bergenia	hybrids pigsqueak
Chelone	turtle-head
Cimicifuga species	bugbane, snakeroot
Eupatorium fistulosum	joe-pye weed
Filipendula rubra	queen-of-the-prairie
Hibiscus moscheutos	swamp mallow
Iris ensata	Japanese iris
Iris pseudacorus	yellow flag iris
Iris versicolor	blue flag iris
Lobellia cardinalis	red cardinal flower
Myosotis sylvatica	woodland forget-me-not
Tradescantia	spiderwort
Trollius europaeus	globeflower

Appendix B
Drought- and Heat-Tolerant Perennials

BOTANICAL NAME	COMMON NAME
Achillea	yarrow
Amsonia tabernaemontana	eastern bluestar
Artemesia	mugwort
Asclepias tuberosa	butterfly weed
Baptisia	false indigo
Callirhoe involucrata	poppy mallow
Cerastium tomentosum	snow-in-summer
Coreopsis verticillata	threadleaf coreopsis
Echinacea	coneflower
Echinops	globe thistle
Eryngium	seaholly
Gaura lindheimeri	Lindheimer's beeblossom
Helianthus	sunflower
Heliopsis	oxeye daisy

BOTANICAL NAME	COMMON NAME
Hemerocallis	daylily
Hibiscus moscheutos	hardy hibiscus
Iris germanica	bearded iris
Leucanthemum nipponicum	Nippon daisy
Leucanthemum × superbum	Shasta daisy
Liatris	gayfeather
Limonium latifolium	sea lavender
Nepeta	catmint
Oenothera	evening primrose
Perovskia	Russian sage
Rudbeckia	black-eyed Susan
Saponaria ocymoides	soapwort
Sedum	stonecrops
Spigella marilandica	Indian pink
Stachys	lamb's ears
Sempervivum tectorum	hens-and-chickens
Thymus	thyme

Appendix C
Grey Foliage Plants

BOTANICAL NAME	COMMON NAME
Achillea 'moonshine'	yarrow
Artemesia ludoviciana	mugwort
Dianthus	pinks
Lamium maculatum	dead nettle
Lavendula	lavender
Lychnis coronaria	campion
Nepeta	catmint
Perovskia atriplicifolia	Russian sage
Ruta graveolens	rue
Salvia	sage
Stachys	lamb's ears
Thymus pseudolanuginosus	woolly thyme
Veronica spicata incana	woolly speedwell

Appendix D
Dark Foliage Plants

BOTANICAL NAME	COMMON NAME	CULTIVAR
Ajuga reptans	Bugleweed	'Bronze Beauty'
Ajuga reptans	Bugleweed	'Chocolate Chip'
Bergenia purpurascnes	Bergenia	'Bressingham Ruby'
Ceratostigma plumbaginoides	Plumbago	
Cimicifuga ramose	Snakeroot	'Brunette'
Geranium macrorrhizum	Bigroot Geranium	
Heuchera micrantha	Coral Bells	'Palace purple', 'Obsidian'
Ligularia dentata	Groundsel	'Britt-Marie Crawford'
Lobelia × speciosa	Cardinal Flower	'Queen Victoria'
Penstemon digitalis	Beardtongue	'Husker Red'
Salvia officinalis	Sage	'Purpurascens'
Sedum	Stonecrop	'Black Jack', 'Dragon's Blood', 'Purple Emperor', 'Voodoo'

Appendix E
Small Bulbs Planted in the Fall, Blooming Early Spring

BOTANICAL NAME	COMMON NAME
Allium sphaerocephalum	drumstick allum
Anemone blanda	Grecian windflower
Chiondoxa luciliae	glory-of-the-snow
Convallaria majalis	lily-of-the-valley
Crocus chrysanthus	snow crocus
Crocus × vernus	large Dutch crocus hybrid
Erathis hyemalis	winter aconite
Erythronium americanum	trout lily
Galanthas nivalis	snowdrops
Iris reticulata	early dwarf iris
Leucojum vernum	spring snowflake (1' tall)
Muscari botryoides	grape hyacinth
Puschkinia scilloides	striped squill
Scilla siberica	Siberian squill
Trillium grandiflorum	showy wildflower
Tulip kaufmanniana	water lily tulip
Tulipa batalinii	Bokhara tulip
Tulipa clusiana	candystick tulip
Tulipa pulchella	dwarf Taurus tulip

Appendix F

Large Spring Bulbs Planted in the Fall, Blooming in the Spring

BOTANICAL NAME	COMMON NAME
Allium caeruleum; A. azureum	blue globe onion (1–3' tall)
Allium schoenoprasum	chive
Camassia leichtlinii	camas
Fritillaria imperalis	crown imperial
Fritillaria meleagris	checkered lily
Hyacinthoides hispanica	wood hyacinth
Hyacinthoides orientalis	Dutch hyacinth
Iris × xiphium	Dutch iris
Narcissus hybrids	daffodils
Narcissus jonquilla	jonquils
Narcissus × poeticus	poet's narcissus, pheasant eye
Tulipa × hybrida	tulip (often not perennial)

Appendix G

Short Herbaceous Perennials for Spring Bloom

BOTANICAL NAME	COMMON NAME
Ajuga reptans	bugleweed
Alchemilla mollis	lady's mantle
Alyssum saxtile	basket-of-gold
Aquilegia × hybrida	columbine
Arabis caucasica	wall rock cress
Bergenia cordifolia	bergenia
Brunnera macrophylla	forget-me-not
Campanula garganica	gargano bell-flower
Campanula portenschlagiana	Dalmatian bellflower
Cerastium tomentosum	snow-in-summer (aggressive)
Chrysogonum virginianum	goldenstar
Corydalis lutea	yellow corydalis
Dianthus deltoides	maiden pink
Dianthus gratianspolitanus	cheddar pink
Dicentra eximia	fringed bleeding heart
Epimedium	barrenwort
Galium odoratum	sweet woodruff
Hedyotis caerulia	bluets (for naturalizing in moist woodlands; aggressive)
Heuchera	coral bells

Iberis sempervirens	candytuft
Iris crestata	crested iris
Lamium maculatum	dead nettle
Phlox divaricata	woodland phlox
Phlox subulata	creeping phlox
Pulmonara angustifolia	lungwort
Sanguinaria canadensis	bloodroot
Saponaria ocymoides	rock soapwort
Thymus praecox	mother-of-thyme
Tiarella cordifolia	foamflower
Viola tricolor	Johnny-jump-up

Appendix H

Taller Herbaceous Perennials for Spring Bloom

BOTANICAL NAME	COMMON NAME
Anchusa azurea	bugloss
Dicentra spectabilis	bleeding heart
Dictamnus	gas plant
Digitalis grandiflora	foxglove
Doronicum	leopard's bane
Euphorbia	cushion spurge
Gaura	gaura
Helleborus orientalis	Lenten rose
Hesperis matronalis	dame's rocket
Iris hybrida	bearded iris (German)
Iris siberica	Siberian iris
Kniphofia uvaria	red hot poker
Lineum perenne	blue flax
Lunaria annua	money plant
Lychnis coronaria	rose campion
Mertensia virginica	Virginia bluebells
Oenothera speciosa	evening primrose
Paeonia lactiflora	peony
Papaver orientale	Oriental poppy
Polemonium caeruleum	Jacob's ladder
Polygonatum biflorum	Solomon's seal
Pulmonaria saccharata	Bethlehem sage
Ruta graveolens	rue
Salvia officinalis	garden sage
Salvia pratensis	meadow sage
Salvia × superba	hybrid blue salvia

Appendix I

Short Perennials for Summer Bloom

BOTANICAL NAME	COMMON NAME	TIME OF BLOOM
Armeria maritima	thrift	early
Astilbe chinensis	'pumila'	late
Astilbe simplicifolia	'aphrodite'	middle to late
Begonia grandis ssp. *evansiana*	hardy begonia	late
Calamintha nepeta	catmint	middle to late
Campanula carpatica	bellflower	early to middle
Centaurea montana	cornflower	middle
Ceratostigma plumbaginoides	plumbago	late
Coreopsis lanceolata	'Goldfink'	early through late
Coreopsis verticillata	'Moonbeam'	middle to late
Corydalis lutea	yellow corydalis	early through late
Geranium cultivars	cranesbills	vary
Hemerocallis hybrids	daylilies	vary
Heuchera micrantha	'Palace Purple'	early
Heuchera sanguinea	coral bells	early
Hibiscus moscheutos	hardy swamp mallow	late
Hosta spp.	hostas	middle to late
Lamium spp. and cultivars	dead nettle	early to late
Lavendulia angustifolia	'Munstead Dwarf' lavender	early
Liriope muscari	lily turf	late
Nepeta × *faassenii*	catmint	early
Origanum vulgare	golden oregano	middle
Phlox stolonifera	woodland phlox (woodlands)	early
Prunella grandiflora	self-heal	early to middle
Pulmonaria saccharata	Bethlehem sage (foliage)	early
Scabiosa	'Pink Mist'	middle to late
Sedum	'Golden Stonecrop'	middle
Sempervivum tectorum	hen and chicks	middle
Stachys	silver carpet, lamb's ears	middle
Stokesia laevis	Stoke's aster	early to middle
Tiarella wherryi	foamflower	early
Veronica prostrata	harebell	early
Veronica specata	'Minuet'	early

COMBINATIONS OF PLANTS

1. Phlox 'Blue Paradise', veronica 'Sunny Border Blue', daylily 'Happy Returns', coneflower (*Echinacea purpurea*) 'Finale White'.

2. For a border with a layered look of short, medium, and tall plants, plant a line of dianthus 'Firewitch' with coreopsis 'Moonbeam' immediately behind. Behind the coreopsis plant *Echinacea* 'Pink Double Delight' or 'Fragrant Angel' (white) and at the very back plant *Perovskia* (Russian sage). These plants also would work well in an island bed with the tall plants in the center surrounded by the medium plants and with short annuals or dianthus used to edge the entire island.

3. A bed makes a strong statement when bold colors are combined. Edge the border with *Geranium* 'Rozanne' or *Nepeta* 'Blue Wonder'. Behind put white phlox 'David' and dark red daylilies such as *Hemerocallis* 'Lady Scarlet' and in the rear combine the purple New England aster 'Hella Lacy', orange *Helenium* 'Flammendes', and monkshood (*Aconitum* 'Spark's Variety'). Additional plants such as both short and tall sedums, white Shasta daisies, and yellow chrysanthemums could be added to increase both impact and bloom time.

Appendix J
Tall Perennials for Summer Bloom

BOTANICAL NAME	COMMON NAME	TIME OF BLOOM
Acanthus spinosus	spiny bear's breeches	early to middle
Achillea filipendulina 'Gold Plate'	yarrow	early through late
Achillea × 'Moonshine'	yarrow	early through late
Alcea rosea 'Old Farmyard'	hollyhock	early to middle
Amsonia montana	blue star	early
Anchusa azura	bugloss	early to middle
Aquilegia × *hybrida*	columbine	early
Aruncus sylvester	goat's beard	early to middle
Asclepias tuberosa	butterfly weed	middle
Astilbe simplicifolia 'Bronze Elegance'	astilbe	middle to late
Astilbe taquetti 'Superba'	astilbe	late
Astilbe × *arendsii* 'Red Sentinel'	astilbe	early to middle
Baptista australis	baptista	early
Campanula glomerata	clustered bellflower	early to middle
Centranthus ruber	red valerian	early
Chelone lyonii	turtle head	late
Chrysanthemum parthenium	feverfew	middle to late
Chrysanthemum × *superbum*	Shasta daisy	early to middle
Dictamnus albus	gas plant	early
Digitalis grandiflora	foxglove	early
Echinacea purpurea	coneflower	middle to late
Echinops ritro	globe thistle	middle

Tall Perennials for Summer Bloom (continued)

BOTANICAL NAME	COMMON NAME	TIME OF BLOOM
Eryngium amethystinum	sea holly	middle to late
Eupatorium coelestinum	hardy ageratum	late
Eupatorium fistulosum	joe-pye weed	late
Filipendula rubra	queen of the prairie	middle
Gaura lindheimeri	white gaura	early through late
Gypsophila paniculata	baby's breath	early to middle
Heliopsis	false sunflower	middle to late
Hemerocallis cultivars		
('Happy Returns' and other re-bloomers)	daylilies	early through late
Hibiscus moscheutos	'Southern Belle' hibiscus	middle
Iris ensata	Japanese iris	middle
Iris hybrida	bearded iris	early to middle
Iris siberica	Siberian iris	early
Kniphofia	red hot poker	early through late
Liatris spicata	gayfeather	middle
Ligularia cultivars	golden ray	middle to late
	(foliage and flowers)	
Lobelia cardinalis	cardinal flower	late
Lobelia siphilitica	big blue lobelia	late
Lychnis coronaria	rose campion	early
Macleaya cordata	plume poppy	middle
Malva alcea	hollyhock mallow	middle to late
Monarda didyma	bee balm	middle
Oenothera speciosa	evening primrose	early
Paeonia lactiflora	peony	early
Penstemon digitalis 'Husker Red'	beard tongue	early
Perovskia	Russian sage	middle to late
Phlox paniculata	summer phlox	middle to late
Physostigia virginiana	obedient plant	middle
Platycodon grandiflorus	balloon flower	middle
Rudbeckia fulgeda	orange coneflower	middle
Ruta graveolens	rue	middle
Salvia × *superba*	blue salvia	early
Sidalcea malviflora	mallow	middle to late
Stachys byzantina	lamb's ears	middle
Thalictrum	mist flower	middle
Thalictrum rochebruneanum	lavender mist or	late
	meadow mist	
Tradescantia × *andersoniana*	spiderwort	late
Tricyrtis hirta	toad lily	late
Verbascum × *hybridum*	mullein	middle to late
Veronica longifolia	speedwell	early to middle
Yucca filamentosa	Adam's needle	middle

Appendix K
Hardy Summer-Blooming Bulbs

BOTANICAL NAME	COMMON NAME
Allium azureum	blue globe onion
Allium sphaerocephalum	drumstick chive
Crocosmia × crocosmiiflora 'Lucifer'	montbretia
Cyclamen hederifolium	hardy cyclamen
Cyclamen neopolitanum	hardy cyclamen (with mulch)
Lilium Asiatic hybrids	Asiatic hybrid lilies
Lilium Oriental hybrids	Oriental hybrid lilies
Lilium × auralianense	aurelian, trumpet lilies
Lycoris squamigera	naked lady, surprise lily

Appendix L
Fall-Flowering Perennials and Bulbs

BOTANICAL NAME	COMMON NAME
Aconitum carmichaelii	azure monkshood
Actaea simplex	snakeroot
Amsonia hubrichtii	Arkansas blue star
Amsonia tabernaemontana	eastern bluestar (yellow foliage in fall; blue flowers in spring)
Anaphalis triplinervis	pearly everlasting
Anemone hybrida	Japanese anemone
Aster novae-angliae	fall aster
Aster × frikartii 'Monch'	fall aster
Astilbe taquetii 'Superba'	fall astilbe
Begonia grandis	hardy begonia
Belamcanda chinenses	blackberry lily
Boltonia asteroides 'Snowbank'	fall daisy
Caryopteris clandonensis	bluebeard shrub
Ceratostigma plumbaginoides	plumbago, leadwort
Chelone lyonii	turtlehead
Chrysanthemum nipponicum	Montauk daisy
Chrysanthemum weyrichii	miyabe mum
Chrysanthemum × morifolium	garden mum
Chrysanthemum × rubellum	daisy mum
Cimicifuga simplex	bugbane
Colchicum autumnale	autumn crocus
Corydalis lutea	yellow corydalis

Fall-Flowering Perennials and Bulbs (continued)

BOTANICAL NAME	COMMON NAME
Crocus sativus	saffron crocus
Crocus spiciosus	fall crocus
Echinacea purpurea	purple coneflower
Eupatorium coelestinum	hardy ageratum
Euphorbia polychroma	spurge (red foliage in fall; yellow flowers earlier)
Gaura lindheimeri	gaura
Geranium 'Rozeanne'	cranesbill
Helenium hybrids	sneezeweed
Helianthus angustifolius	swamp sunflower
Helianthus multiflorus 'Flora-Pleno'	double sunflower
Hemerocallis hybrids	re-blooming daylily
Iris hybrida	bearded re-blooming iris
Lespedeza	Thunbergii bush clover (6')
Liriope 'Silvery Sunproof'	lilyturf
Lobelia siphilitica	great blue lobelia
Malva alcea	hollyhock mallow
Perovskia atriplicifolia	Russian sage
Rudbeckia fulgida	orange coneflower
Rudbeckia nitida	shining coneflower
Sedum cauticolum 'Ruby Glow'	stonecrop
Sedum hybrids	stonecrop
Sedum × telephium 'Autumn Joy'	stonecrop
Solidago hybrids	goldenrod
Tricyrtis hirta	toad lily
Veronicastrum virginicum	culver's root

Appendix M
Deer-Resistant Plants

Although deer seem to eat anything if they are hungry enough, aromatic plants don't seem to attract them so readily. Try these if Bambi is not your favored garden guest:

columbine	lamb's ears	plumbago
daffodils	lavender	Russian sage
euphorbia	lily of the valley	salvia
grape hyacinths	monarda	veronica
hellebore	nepeta	
iris	peony	

Appendix N
Self-Seeding Annuals to Combine with Perennials

NAME	COMMENTS
Alyssum	Low-growing with lacy white flower heads
Cosmos	Medium and tall with single flowers in pink, white, and rose shades
larkspur	Tall airy plants with violet blue, white, pink, purple, and bi-color flowers
Nicotiana	Medium and tall varieties and white, pink, or red flowers. *N. sylvestris* is the tallest, with large tobacco leaves
Nigella	Medium-sized plant with pink, white, and blue flowers and interesting seed pods
poppies	Tall plants with single or double flowers
Salvia farinacea 'Victoria'	Medium-sized plant with blue flower spikes that retain color when dried. An annual in areas with cold winters

Appendix O
Perennials That Flower in Shade

NAME	COLORS
Begonia grandis (hardy begonia)	pink
Dicentra eximia (bleeding heart)	pink
Epimedium (bishop's hat)	yellow, pink, and white
Galium odoratum (sweet woodruff)	white ground cover
Helleborus (Lenten rose)	chartreuse, white, purple wine
Hosta	white and lavender
Lamium (dead nettle)	pink, lavender, white
Liriope muscari (lilyturf)	blue or white (edging plant)
Polygonatum (Solomon's seal)	white
Pulmonaria (lungwort)	blue, white, and pink
Tricyrtis (toad lily)	varied and speckled
Vinca minor (periwinkle)	blue (ground cover)

Appendix P
Blue and Purple Perennials

Adenophora liliifolia
Zones 3–8

Tall with vertical flower spikes made up of nodding bells. Easy to grow in any soil and spreads rapidly. It blooms from summer to fall and does well in sun or part shade.

Agastache
'Blue Fortune'
Zones 5–10

Tall, clump-forming anise hyssop with aromatic foliage and blue flower spires attractive to hummingbirds and butterflies. Self-seeds, and seeds are attractive to goldfinches. Likes good drainage and blooms from summer to fall in sun.

Anchusa
'Dropmore'
Zones 3–8

Tall plant with upright clusters of intense blue small flowers. Prefers good drainage and may be cut to the ground after blooming. It blooms in late spring to early summer in sun.

Aquilegia
Colorado columbine
Zones 3–8

Medium-height blue-green-leaved plants with dainty flowers blooming in late spring in sun to part shade. Self-seeds in a restrained way.

Aster frikartii
'Wonder of Staffa'
Zones 5–8

Medium-height airy mounds of lavender-blue flowers with yellow centers from July until a hard freeze. Blooms well in full sun. Comparable to A. 'Monch'.

Aster novae-angliae
'Purple Dome'
Zones 3–8

A short form of the tall New England aster that forms robust clumps with clusters of starry little daisy-type flowers from later summer to fall in sun.

Aster novi-belgii
'Eventide'
Zones 3 8

Tall, dark blue New York aster. Pinch back and divide like mums; durable and long-lived with blooms in fall in sun. 'Raydon's Favorite' and the short 'October Skies' are excellent also.

Astilbe
'Amethyst'
Zones 4–8

Moisture-loving plant with ferny foliage. This is a medium-height early-summer-blooming cultivar with plumes of lavender when planted in shade to part sun. A. *chinensis* 'Pumila' is a short, late-blooming lavender that spreads well.

Aubretia
'Novalis Blue'
Zones 5–8

Short, mat-forming grey-green plant covered with true-blue flowers that grows in rock gardens and walls. It blooms in the spring in sun to part shade.

Baptisia australis
'Purple Smoke'
Zones 3–9

A tall, clump-forming, long-lived plant that needs room to spread to 3'; has handsome blue-green foliage, lupine-like flower spikes, and dark, interesting seed pods for dried arrangements. It blooms in spring in sun to part shade.

Boltonia asteroides
'Nana'
Zones 4–9

A lower-growing, pale blue variety of the tall boltonia with masses of starry little flowers all fall in sun or part shade. Use in front of the taller B. 'Snowbank', which is white and never needs staking.

Brunnera macrophylla
Zones 3–7

A short, 16" plant with dark green heart-shaped leaves and clusters of small sky-blue flowers in woodland settings. B. 'Jack Frost' is a cultivar with silver leaves.

Campanula glomerata
'Joan Eliot'
Zones 3–8

Violet-blue clusters of flowers face upwards on 14" plants that bloom late spring to early summer. They like a moderately rich, well-drained soil, and sun to light shade.

Campanula poscharskyana
'Blue Waterfall'
Zones 4–7

A vigorous creeper, this low-growing plant is ideal for rock gardens, window boxes, and walls. It likes sun or part shade and blooms in the summer.

Centaurea montana Zones 3–8	Medium-sized plants with blue cornflowers which will repeat if plants are cut back after the first flush. C. 'Purple Heart' is hardy and drought-tolerant.
Echinops 'Ritro' 'Taplow Blue' Zones 3–8	Tall, carefree globe thistles with handsome leaves, late summer ball-shaped flowers, and an architectural habit in sun.
Eryngium 'Sapphire Blue' Zones 5–9	A medium to tall plant that blooms in summer with architectural branching stems, domed flowers, and stiff spiky leaves. The steely blue-grey is best in full sun with good drainage, and the flowers are excellent for fresh or dried arrangements.
Geranium cinereum 'Purple Pillow' Zones 5–8	Mounded, low-growing plants flowering across the summer into fall, when the foliage turns bronze. G. 'Rozanne' also is blue with red fall foliage.
Lavandula angustifolia 'Granny's Bonnet' Zones 5–7	A compact 16" tough lavender with spikes of deep violet flowers, upright habit, and long flower season during the summer; needs good drainage and sun. L. 'Blue Cushion' also has a compact habit.
Lobelia L. *siphilitica* (blue) Zones 4–8	Tall blue lobelia that likes a moist woodland setting. Tall, narrow spikes of flowers, adaptable in most growing situations.
Nepeta 'Blue Wonder' (12") 'Dropmore Hybrid' (18") 'Six Hills Giant' (3') Zones 3–8	Short and tall plants with grey foliage. Cut back for re-bloom. Long flowering and blue or violet flowers.
Penstemon P. *angustifolius* Zones 3–8	A native plant with tubular flowers that prefers hot, dry conditions. This 12" variety self-seeds well and prefers sun.
Perovskia P. *atriplicifolia* (3') Zones 4–9	Flowers for two months from summer into fall. Drought-tolerant with silver-grey foliage and spikes of small blue flowers. Do not cut back these tall statuesque plants further than 12" in the fall.
Phlox divaricata 'Blue Moon' Zones 3–8	Native blue woodland phlox. A spreading early bloomer, 12" high.
Phlox paniculata 'Blue Paradise' 'David's Lavender' Zones 4–8	Tall plants that flower in midsummer in full sun. Mildew-resistant varieties.
Phlox subulata Zones 3–9	Lavender creeping phlox that spreads in sunny spots and drapes well on walls and slopes.
Platycodon 'Mariesii' Zones 3–9	An 18" long-lived plant with blue, bell-shaped blossoms and puffy buds, growing in sun or part shade. Long-lived but slow to emerge in spring.
Polemonium 'Blue Pearl' Zones 4–8	A short Jacob's Ladder, this is a long-lived blue flowering plant with attractive foliage. Does well in part shade.
Pulmonaria longifolia 'Bertram Anderson' Zones 3–8	Short shade plant with mounding habit and handsome foliage in a woodland setting. Dark blue flowers and silver-spotted leaves.

Blue and Purple Perennials (continued)

Salvia
   'East Friesland'
   'May Night'
   Zones 4–8

All varieties grow well in full sun and are deer-resistant. Medium to tall plants that can be cut back to encourage re-bloom.

Scabiosa Columbaria
   'Butterfly Blue'
   Zones 4–8

Short, long-flowering plants with blue-grey foliage in full sun or part shade.

Stokesia
   'Purple Parasols'
   Zones 5–9

Long-flowering 18" plants that need some protection in northern gardens. Flowers change from powdery blue through magenta as they mature, summer to fall.

Thymus
   'Elfin'
   Zones 3–9

Short creeping thyme needs good drainage and has hairy leaves and miniature flowers in the spring. Grows in sun or part shade.

Veronica
   'Blue Carpet' (8–10")
   'Sunny Border Blue' (2')
   'Waterperry Blue' (5")
   Zones 3–8

Short to medium-height plants that like well-drained soil in full to part sun.

Viola
   'Royal Robe'
   Zones 4–8

Large flowering violets on short 6–8" plants that self-sow in sun and part shade. Fragrant flowers in spring and early summer.

Appendix Q

Pink, Red, and White Perennials

Achillea ptarmica
   'The Pearl'
   Zones 4–8

A two-foot plant with a white double flower that is different from other achilleas and more restrained in the garden. 'Summerwine' is red, and all achilleas thrive in sun.

Agastache
   'Heather Queen'
   'Cona'
   Zones 5–8

Tall, adaptable hyssops with pink blossoms attractive to butterflies and hummingbirds. Need good drainage and sun.

Anemone
   'Honorine Jobert' (white)
   'Elegans' (pink)
   Zones 5–8

Tall Japanese anemones that need winter protection in northern states and bloom late summer through fall in sun and part shade. Grow them where they can spread.

Aquilegia hybrids
   'Songbird Cardinal'
   Zones 3–8

Graceful medium-sized plants with red and white bi-color flowers that last well in a vase. Spring and summer bloom in sun and part shade.

Arabis caucasica
   'Snowcap'
   'Red Sensation'

Short 8" spring bloomers that grow in sun or shade and are excellent for edging. Flower in spring.

Aster
   'Alma Postschke' (pink, medium)
   'Harrington's Pink' (pink, tall)
   'Snow Cushion' (white, short)
   Zones 3–8

Provide color in the fall garden and are adaptable and long-lived. They do best in sun and are not fussy about soil conditions.

Astilbe
  'Bridal Veil' (28")
  'Sprite' (12")
  'Fire' (36")
  Zones 4–8

These plants have ferny foliage, bloom in shade, and come in whites, reds, and pinks, blooming across a long season.

Bergenia
  'Winterglow'
  Zones 3–8

Short plants with glossy heart-shaped leaves and bright pink flowers in spring in sun and part shade.

Boltonia asteroides
  'Snowbank' (3–5')
  'Pink' (3')
  Zones 3–9

Tall, fall-blooming sturdy plants that are good companions for asters and grow well anywhere in full sun.

Campanula
  'Cherry Bells'
  Zones 4–8

Vigorous medium-high plant with tubular cherry-red flowers in summer. Spreads in fertile soil in sun and part shade. 'Lactiflora' is a dwarf pink.

Centranthus
  'Ruber'
  'Abbus'
  Zones 5–8

A 2–3' plant that blooms from June till frost above low green foliage in sun or part shade.

Cimicifuga racemosa
  Zones 3–8

Very tall white spires on plants with low, attractive foliage in sun or part shade. Blooms in late summer.

Dianthus
  'Fire Witch' (red)
  'Bath's Pink'
  Zones 3–8

Short, scented flowers on heat-tolerant plants with blue-green foliage. They grow in sun or part shade.

Dicentra spectabilis
  'Rosea'
  'Alba'
  Zones 3–8

Medium 28" plants with pendulous flowers on stems held above attractive foliage that dies down after spring bloom. Plant in sun and part shade.

Epimedium youngianum
  'White Star'
  Zones 5–9

Good ground cover for shade with delicate blooms in spring.

Filipendula hexapetala
  'Flora Plena'
  Zones 3–10

A tall plant with elegant foliage and white feathery plumes in late spring and early summer. Likes moisture but tolerates drought.

Gaura lindheimeri
  Zones 5–9

Tall heat- and humidity-resistant plant with white airy flowers in spring and early fall in sun.

Geranium macrorrhizum
  Zones 4–8

Blooms May through June with pink, white, and magenta flowers and red foliage in the fall. It adapts to sun or shade and is low-growing and drought-tolerant and a good ground cover.

Heuchera hybrids
  'Freedom'
  Zones 4–10

A 24" plant with a pink flower spike that rises above striking foliage. 'Freedom' is usually the last heuchera to stop flowering.

Heucherella
  'Rosalie'
  Zones 4–8

A cross between heuchera and tiarella that forms a ground cover and flowers spring/summer with repeating into fall. Dainty pastel flowers on 6–18" plants in part shade.

Iris cristata
  Zones 5–9

A short white native iris that likes moist humus-rich soil with a neutral pH and regular division.

Pink, Red, and White Perennials (continued)

Lamium
'White Nancy'
'Beacon Silver'
Zones 3–8

Short ground cover plants with white striped foliage, growing in sun or shade and tolerating drought, with spring/summer bloom.

Lobelia
'Cardinalis'
'Ruby Slipper'
Zones 3–8

A tall lobelia with red flower spires in late summer and fall. Likes moist soil in part or full shade.

Lychnis
'Rose Campion'
Zones 5–7

Red blooms on plants with silvery foliage of medium height in sun or part shade.

Lychnis chalcedonica
'Maltese Cross'
Zones 3–8

A tall plant with scarlet flower heads in summer. Good cut flower and green, upright growth in sun.

Malva alcea
'Fastigiata'
Zones 4–9

A tall plant with pink flowers summer through fall in sun to partial shade. Short-lived, but self-sows. Cut back to prolong bloom.

Oenothera speciosa
'Siskiyou'
Zones 5–9

A short plant for sun and poor, dry soils, as it is aggressive in rich soils. Blooms with pink flowers all summer and provides a colorful ground cover.

Papaver orientalis
'Beauty of Livermore' (red)
'Princess Victoria Louise' (pink)
Zones 3–8

Tall plant with paper-thin petalled blooms held aloft in early summer in sunny spots. Does not like to be moved.

Penstemon digitalis
'Husker Red'
'Alba'
Zones 3–9

Medium-tall upright plants with attractive foliage and pink or white flowers in summer in sun.

Phlox paniculata
'David' (white)
'Starfire' (red)
'Pinafore' (pink)
Zones 4–8

Tall, late summer–blooming plants with fragrant clustered flower heads, in sunny locations.

Physostegia virginiana
'Miss Manners' (white)
'Pink Bouquet'
Zones 3–9

Tall, late summer bloomers with many flower spikes. They are drought-resistant but aggressive in moist soil. Enjoy sun or part shade and make good cut flowers.

Saponaria ocymoides
Zones 3–8

Short creeping plant with profuse pink bloom in late spring in sun.

Sedum
'Matrona'
'Brilliant'
'Dragonsblood'
Zones 3–9

Tall 1½' plants with self-supporting stems, colorful foliage, and broad, dusty-pink flowers that persist into fall. Short 12" branching 'Dragonsblood' is a succulent with red foliage and pink or red flowers.

Veronica
'Minuet' (pink)
'Raspberry Ice'
Zones 4–10

Grows well in well-drained soil in full to part sun with pink or red flower spires in summer. 'Red Fox' tolerates shade.

Appendix R

Yellow and Orange Perennials

Achillea
  'Coronation Gold'
  'Moonshine'
  'Terra Cotta'
  Zones 3–9

Tall, tough, heat- and drought-tolerant summer bloomers.

Agastache
  'Apache Sunset'
  Zones 5–8

A 20" plant that blooms in the sun from June to October.

Alyssum compactum
  Zones 4–8

Bright yellow flowers cover low plants with grey-green foliage in spring in sun to part shade.

Aquilegia chrysantha
  Zones 3–9

This tall yellow native columbine grows up to 3–4' and flowers from late spring to late summer, tolerating both heat and shade. Plants grown in full sun, however, will bloom more and be more compact in zones 3–9.

Asclepias tuberosa
  Zones 3–9

This butterfly weed thrives in drought and is 18–24" tall with orange umbels of flowers in summer.

Baptisia sphaerocarpa
  Zones 4–9

An alternative to lupins, these yellow pea-shaped flower spikes tolerate drought, humidity, and cold winters and grow 2–3' with summer blooms in sun or part shade.

Centaurea macrocephala
  Zones 4–8

A tall plant with coarse leaves and bright yellow thistle flowers in sun in summer.

Chrysogonum virginianum
  'Yellow Star'

This 4" ground cover has scalloped leaves and grows in sun to part shade, bearing bright yellow flowers spring to summer. Ideal for moist wildflower gardens.

Coreopsis
  'Crème Brule'
  Zones 4–9

Similar to 'Moonbeam' but with larger, darker yellow flowers that bloom from summer into fall in sun.

Coreopsis verticillata
  'Early Sunrise'
  Zones 5–9

A double-flowered coreopsis that blooms in sun, summer through fall.

Digitalis purpurea
  'Apricot Beauty'
  Zones 5–9

Pastel shades of apricot flowers in the summer in part shade. Grows 4' tall.

Doronicum orientale
  Zones 4–8

A spring bloomer with yellow flowers, growing in shade and part sun. Plant in moist soil under trees.

Echinacea
  'Sunrise' (yellow)
  'Sunset' (orange)
  'Summer Sky' (orange/pink)
  Zones 3–9

New varieties of the purple coneflower but with the original carefree habit. Grow in sun in groups up to 30" tall.

Euphorbia polychroma

A 14" plant that has chrome yellow bracts in early summer that turn red in fall. Grows in sun or part shade.

Yellow and Orange Perennials (continued)

Gaillardia
'Oranges and Lemons'
Zones 3–10

An 18" easily grown blanket flower with golden orange flowers from early summer through fall in sun. Tolerates heat, drought, and humidity.

Helenium
'Mardi Gras'
Zones 4–8

A tall late-summer bloomer with yellow, orange, and red flowers in sun.

Heliopsis
'Bressingham Doubloon'
Zones 4–9

A very tall late-summer performer for the back of the border. Plant in sun.

Heliopsis
'Summer Sun'
Zones 3–8

A 3' plant that flowers in sun from midsummer into fall. A good flower for cutting.

Hemerocallis
'Stella d'Oro'
'Happy Returns'
'Mini Stella'
Zones 3–9

Short, repeat-bloom daylilies in yellow shades that make an excellent edging or ground cover. Not troubled by pests. Plant with daffodils for a long bloom progression.

Heuchera
'Amber Waves'
Zones 3–8

Amber-colored clumps of decorative foliage with cream flowers in late spring, growing in sun or part shade. Can form a ground cover under deciduous trees.

Kniphofia unvaria
'Flamenco'
Zones 5–9

A plant 30" tall, with spikes of red, orange, yellow, and cream flowers in summer.

Lingularia dentata
'The Rocket' (yellow)
'Desdemona' (orange)
Zones 5–8

Tall plants with big leaves that do best with moisture and some shade. Summer flower spikes provide a dramatic presence in the shade garden.

Liriope
'Pee Dee Ingot'

A short ground cover or edging plant with vivid yellow leaves that mature to gold/chartreuse. Lavender flowers in spring in part shade.

Oenothera speciosa
'Sunset Boulevard'
Zones 5–9

A medium-short evening primrose with flowers in sun in summer. Flowers open late in the day and close in the morning. Plant in well-drained poor soil, as it is aggressive in rich soil.

Papaver orientalis
'Coral Reef'
Zones 3–8

Medium to tall plants blooming in late spring in sun.

Rudbeckia hirta
'Irish Eyes'
Zones 3–6

A medium-tall plant with yellow daisy flowers with green centers. Blooms in summer and fall in sun.

Rudbeckia species
'Goldsturm'
Zones 3–9

All rudbeckias are robust plants with tall stature, unbothered by insects or drought. 'Goldsturm' is an award-winner. Summer bloom in sun.

Sedum
'Kamtschaticum'
Zones 3–10

Short, fleshy plants with scalloped leaves and yellow flowers in summer, maturing to bronze. Grow in sun.

Sedum
'Autumn Fire'
'Autumn Joy'
Zones 3–9

Medium-tall plants with reddish flower heads in fall that combine well with asters and chrysanthemums. Plant in sun.

Solidago 'Golden Fleece' Zones 4–8	Plants grow to 18" and flower in late summer. Combine well with purple asters. Cut for bouquets before flowers open fully. Most other solidagos are very tall.
Trollius ledebourii 'Golden Queen' Zones 3–7	This 2' globeflower needs rich, moist soil and part shade to produce its globular orange blossoms.
Verbascum chaixii 'Sixteen Candles' Zones 3–9	A tall, erect plant that needs full sun to produce gold flowers with violet filaments over a basal rosette of leaves that look like grey felt.
Vinca minor 'Illumination'	A ground cover with green-edged golden foliage and blue flowers in spring in shade to part sun.

Appendix S
Exposure and Siting Plants

Points to Remember

- Southern and western exposures in your garden will get the most sun and warmth. Your bulbs that are planted on the south side, for example, will get the morning sun, and so will probably be the first to bloom in your garden in the spring, especially if you plant some early-blooming varieties.
- Plants growing near structures such as buildings, walls, fences, and shrubs will get more protection than those in an open space.
- Low areas will be more susceptible to frost than those on either the tops or sides of hills, as cold air moves downwards. Those plants that are in low frost pockets will suffer more during freezing and thawing in early spring, and some plants are more susceptible to this than others.
- Periods of gusting winds will dry out the soil and plants may be damaged, so mulch heavily. Plants in pots always dry out more than plants in the ground.
- Arches and pergolas planted with vines will cast shade and also provide some protection for plants beneath.
- Hostas will light up dark corners and cover unattractive muddy areas and stifle the proliferation of weeds.
- Tender summer-blooming bulbs that are dug in the fall can be placed in newspaper in a dry (above freezing) garage or basement during the winter for replanting next spring.
- Limb up deciduous trees with low-hanging branches to provide more light for the shade-loving plants under them.

Appendix T

More on Nomenclature

Flower	*anthus*	
	florus	
Flower characteristics	*florepleno*	full flowers
	floribundus	many blooms
	glomeratus	clustered
	grandiflorus	large blooms
	pleniflorus	double blooms
Colors	*albus*	white
	argenteus	silver
	chrysanthis	golden
	flavissimus	very yellow
	flavovirens galbinus	greenish yellow
	flavus	yellow
	fulvus	tawny
	fumidus	smoky grey
	fuscus	swarthy
	pallidus	pale
	rubrus	red
	violaceus	violet
	virens	green
Leaves	*folius*	
	phyllus	
Leaf characteristics	*filifolius*	thread-like leaves
	foliatus	full of leaves
	gladiatus	like a sword
	glaucifolius	grey leaves
	grandifolius	large leaves
	hebephyllus	downy leaves
	hederifolius	ivy-shaped leaves
	hibiscifolius	leaves like the hibiscus
	hirsutus	hairy
	ilicifolius	leaves like holly
Origins	*chinensis*	China
	floridanus	Florida
	formosanus	Formosa, now Taiwan
	gallicus	France
	germanicus	Germany
	japonica	Japan
	orientalis	the East

Additional characteristics	*cristatus*	crested
	divaricatus	spreading
	edulis	edible
	fastigiatus	erect branches
	ferreus	fiercely thorny
	foetidus	bad-smelling
	fragrans	scented
	officinalis	medicinal
	prostratus	lying on the ground

Appendix U
Lessons Learned in a Garden in the Lower Midwest

- Use lamb's ears (*Stachys byzantina* 'Big Ears') as an edging or ground cover. They tolerate heat and humidity and are short (10" tall) with big grey velvety leaves and few flowers, so there are fewer spent heads to cut down. Zones 4–8 in sunny, well-drained spots.

- For tall exuberant color, plant oxeye daisy (*Heliopsis helianthoides* 'Sommersonne'), which grows 2–4 feet tall and has profuse yellow blooms in mid- to late summer. It is cheerful planted *en masse* and displayed in a vase during the dog days of summer. Zones 4–9.

- If you have room for only one short mounded perennial, plant hardy geranium 'Rozanne', with violet flowers with white centers and 20-inch mounds of pretty foliage. It is heat-tolerant but likes regular moisture and afternoon shade in zones 4–7.

- Deer do not like peonies, so if you have deer make a peony walk and use peonies lavishly in mass plantings. Since they live a long time, take care to amend the soil before planting and plant rhizomes with many buds (or eyes) an inch below the surface of the soil. Use them as a buffer around areas where you plant less deer-resistant species. Use wire supports that allow the peonies to grow up through the rings so the plants are kept erect when heavy with bloom.

- Clematis flowering vines should be pruned when dormant if they are fall bloomers so they have lots of time to form new growth on which to bloom. Cut them back to 3 feet. Mid-season bloomers must be pruned early also, but only back to the top set of green buds as soon as they can be identified in the very early spring. Since the early-season ones bloom on old wood, prune them immediately *after* they have bloomed and never later than July.

- A long-blooming low-grower to plant is the yellow-flowering *Corydalis lutea*, but the blue-flowering types are not as satisfactory. Plant this ferny-leaved little gem in moist and shady locations; if it is happy, it is a delightful self-sower.

- Tender summer bulbs, such as dahlia, gladiolus, and calla lily, can be planted in pots so that gardeners in cold climates avoid having to dig them every year. They can be wintered over in a cool but not freezing spot and placed outside again for the next growing season. Annuals in pots, such as coleus, can be cut back hard and wintered over in the house. Rooting a few cuttings of favorites, however, is often easier and takes up less space.

Lessons Learned (continued)

- White hydrangeas are good choices in regions where there is a lot of freezing and thawing in the spring. This damages the buds in those varieties (many of the coveted blues) that bloom on old wood. Those with white flowers bloom on new wood later in the season and so are not affected. Newer colored varieties that bloom on *both* old and new wood are also good choices (including *H.* 'Endless Summer' and 'Blushing Bride'). Do not prune the dead wood off before the plant has leafed out and it is easily identified.
- Tall plants that enjoy clay soil include amsonia, baptisia, liatris, goldenrod, and coneflower.
- If a plant does not thrive, move it and amend the soil before replanting. Give it three chances (that is, three moves) before giving up, as by then you will be exhausted and so will the plant.
- Keep a garden journal so that you remember what you don't want to forget.

Appendix V
Mail Order Resources

www.avantgardensne.com
www.bluestoneperennials.com
www.bussegardens.com
www.everlastingfarm.com
www.gilberthwild.com
www.heronswood.com
www.jungseed.com
www.northwindperennialfarm.com
www.perennialpleasures.net
www.perennialresources.com
www.plantdelights.com
www.theknockoutrose.com
www.waysidegardens.com
www.whiteflowerfarm.com
www.woodlanders.net

Bibliography

Bailey, L. H., and E. Z. Bailey. *Hortus Third: A Concise Dictionary of Plants Cultivated in the United States and Canada*. Rev. ed. New York: McMillan, 1976.

Brown, J. *The Pursuit of Paradise*. London: Harper Collins, 1999.

Ellis, B. W. *Taylor's Guide to Perennials*. New York: Houghton Mifflin, 2000.

Harstad, C. *Go Native: Gardening with Native Plants and Wildflowers in the Lower Midwest*. Bloomington: Indiana University Press, 1999.

———. *Got Shade? A "Take It Easy" Approach for Today's Gardener*. Bloomington: Indiana University Press, 2003.

Loewer, P. *Thoreau's Garden*. Mechanicsburg, Pa.: Stackpole Books, 2002.

Massingham, B. *Gertrude Jekyll*. Aylesbury, Bucks.: Shire Publications, [1975] 1992.

Neal, B. *Gardener's Latin*. Chapel Hill, N.C.: Algonquin Books, 1992.

Roth, S. *A Complete Guide to Flower Gardening*. Des Moines, Iowa: Better Homes and Gardens Books, 1995.

Stearn, W. T. *Botanical Latin*. 4th ed. Portland, Ore.: Timber Press, 1998.

Stewart, A. *Flower Confidential: The Good, the Bad, and the Beautiful in the Business of Flowers*. Chapel Hill, N.C.: Algonquin Books, 2007.

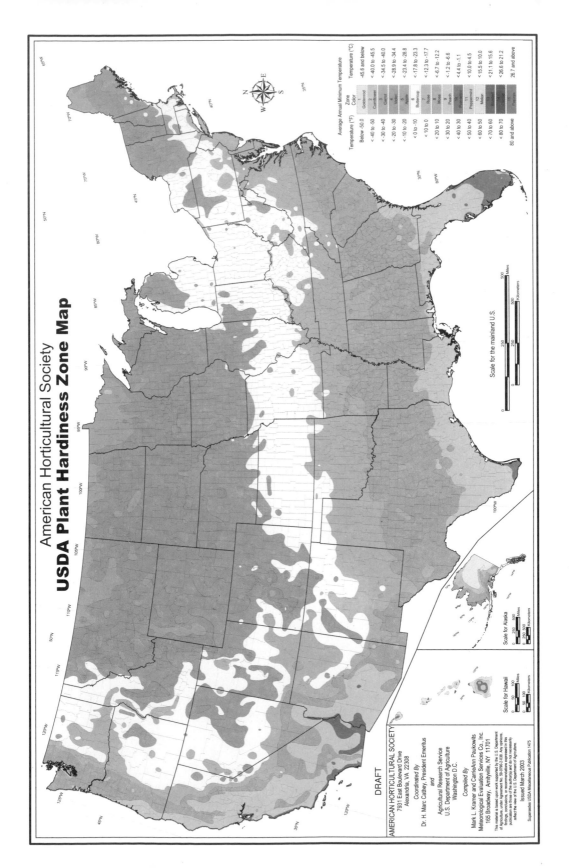

American Horticultural Society
USDA Plant Hardiness Zone Map

DRAFT

AMERICAN HORTICULTURAL SOCIETY
7931 East Boulevard Drive
Alexandria, VA. 22308

Coordinated By
Dr. H. Marc Cathey, President Emeritus
and
Agricultural Research Service
U.S. Department of Agriculture
Washington D.C.

Compiled By
Mark L. Kramer and CarrieAnn Paukowits
Meteorological Evaluation Services Co., Inc.
165 Broadway, Amityville, NY 11701

Issued March 2003

This material is based upon work supported by the U.S. Department
of Agriculture, under Agreement No. 59-0790-2-038. Any opinions,
findings, conclusions, or recommendations expressed in this
publication are those of the author/s and do not necessarily
reflect the view of the U.S. Department of Agriculture.

Supersedes USDA Miscellaneous Publication 1475

Average Annual Minimum Temperature

Temperature (°F)	Zone	Color	Temperature (°C)
Below -50.0	1 Goldenrod		-45.6 and below
-40 to -50	2 Cornflower		-40.0 to -45.5
-30 to -40	3 Carrot		-34.5 to -40.0
-20 to -30	4 Violet		-28.9 to -34.4
-10 to -20	5 Aspen		-23.4 to -28.8
0 to -10	6 Buttercup		-17.8 to -23.3
10 to 0	7 Rose		-12.3 to -17.7
20 to 10	8 Moss		-6.7 to -12.2
30 to 20	9 Prairie		-1.2 to -6.6
40 to 30	10 Periwinkle		4.4 to -1.1
50 to 40	11 Peppermint		10.0 to 4.5
60 to 50	12 Melon		15.5 to 10.0
70 to 60	13		21.1 to 15.6
80 to 70			26.6 to 21.2
80 and above			26.7 and above

Scale for the mainland U.S.

Scale for Hawaii

Scale for Alaska

Index

Photo by Tom Stio, reprinted courtesy of *Bloom Magazine*

A native of Australia, Moya L. Andrews recently retired from an administrative position at Indiana University as Vice Chancellor for Academic Affairs and Dean of the Faculties. She is Professor Emerita of Speech and Hearing Sciences and a prolific author, with numerous research articles and books in her field to her credit and three co-edited volumes, most recently *The Scholarship of Teaching and Learning in Higher Education: Contributions of Research Universities* (Indiana University Press, 2004), with William E. Becker. A Master Gardener, Andrews hosts a weekly radio show, "Focus on Flowers," on WFIU, the NPR affiliate in Bloomington, Indiana. She also writes gardening articles for *Bloom Magazine* in Bloomington.

Gillian Harris, a Bloomington resident and natural science illustrator, has been involved in the study and preservation of the Indiana environment since returning to the area twenty years after graduating from Indiana University. She is an Indiana Master Naturalist and has recently served as president of the South-Central chapter of the Indiana Native Plant and Wildflower Society (INPAWS).

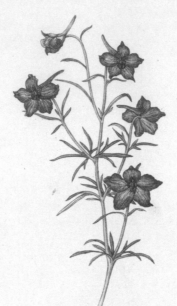

SPONSORING EDITOR
Linda Oblack

MANAGING EDITOR
Miki Bird

PRODUCTION DIRECTOR
Bernadette Zoss

BOOK AND JACKET DESIGN
Pamela Rude

COMPOSITION
Pamela Rude and Tony Brewer

Library of Congress Cataloging-in-Publication Data

Andrews, Moya L.
Perennials short and tall : a seasonal progression of
flowers for your garden / Moya L. Andrews ;
Illustrated by Gillian Harris.
p. cm.
Includes bibliographical references and index.
ISBN 978-0-253-21976-3 (pbk : alk. paper)
1. Perennials—Middle West. I. Title.
SB434.A53 2008
635.9'320978—dc22
2007040048